The Buddha

And the Essence of Dhamma

by

Anand S. Krishna

Empty Canvas Publishers

Empty Canvas Publishers™

Corporate Office:
EMPTY CANVAS PUBLISHERS™
4435-36/7, 1st Floor
Ansari Road, Daryaganj
New Delhi-110002
Email: emptycanvaspublishers@gmail.com

Registered Office:
EMPTY CANVAS PUBLISHERS™
AP-119C, Pitam Pura
New Delhi-110034 (India)
www.emptycanvaspublishers.com

Edition : 2022

ISBN: 978-93-90594-27-6

The Buddha and the Essence of Dhamma

Author : Anand S. Krishna

Illustration: Anand S.Krishna, 2022

Cover Designed by : Scratchpad

Published by:
EMPTY CANVAS PUBLISHERS™
New Delhi-110034 (India)

Processed And Printed in India

Dedicated to

The entire chain of Vipassana Teachers Who preserved and spread the Dhamma in its pristine purity in spite of various difficulties.

"There are beings without limit,
let us take the vow to convey them all across.

There are depravities in us without number, let us take the vow, To extinguish them all,

There are truths without end,
let us take the vow to comprehend them all.

There is the Way of Buddha without comparison, let us take the vow to accomplish it perfectly."

Contents

A Buddhist is not a slave to any body

"A Buddhist is not a slave to a book or to any person. Nor does he sacrifice his freedom of thought by becoming a follower of the Buddha. He can exercise his own free will and develop his knowledge even to the extent of attaining Buddhahood himself, for all are potential Buddhas."

Ven. Narada Maha Thera

in

"What is Buddhism"

Preface

I am delighted to present the book *The Buddha and the Essence of Dhamma* to my readers. The world is passing through great changes today. With the advancement of technology, the entire world has become a global village. The increased flow of money into our hands has increased, raising the standard of our living to unprecedented levels. We have enough material comforts, but the same cannot be said when it comes to the level of mental comfort. Take some random statistics from the office of a psychiatrist; you will see that tension is only increasing in our lives. The gap between the rich and the poor is ever increasing across the globe. Various national governments are spending billions of dollars to stockpile weapons of mass destruction instead of eradicating poverty and unemployment, which are on the rise. But ironically, despite all this preparedness at national defence, people across the globe are feeling more and more insecure due to violence and terrorism which have become everyday phenomena. Under these circumstances, more and more people are drawing solace from spirituality. This return to spirituality is more pronounced in Western societies, which have been known more for their materialistic way of life, thanks to the unprecedented economic prosperity these nations have been enjoying for centuries. Again, this re- embrace of spirituality is more pronounced as they are seeking solace more from the Oriental faiths, especially from the Buddhist teachings. This is not limited to the downtrodden or those living on the fringes of the society, it also includes those who are well off.

As this spiritual revival takes its root, the teachings of the Buddha are also being revisited today with a vigour not seen in the past. More than 2,550 years ago, the Buddha preached the message of compassion, morality, fraternity, non violence, peaceful co-existence, mastery over mind and direct experiential wisdom, which is only too relevant today. Having realised the uselessness and meaninglessness of luxuries and the fleeting nature of the world and its objects, this young prince of Kapilavatthu renounced worldly life to become the Buddha. He attained Enlightenment at the prime age of thirty-five. With infinite love and compassion, he preached *Dhamma* for forty- five years and achieved *Mahāparinibbāna* at the age of eighty.

The Government of India celebrated the 2550th year of *Mahāparinibbāna* of the Buddha as a year-long celebration from the Buddha Pūrṇimā of 2006 to the Buddha Pūrṇimā of 2007. Dr Ambedkar with half a million of his followers embraced Buddhism in 1956. Millions of people across India have celebrated the Golden Jubilee of the *Dhamma* revolution to commemorate the 50th year of Dr. Ambedkar's conversion to Buddhism. According to a report in *The Times of India* (New Delhi dated 10.11.2006), a stupendous three million converted to Buddhism in 2006 itself in the country. And this is not limited to India alone. An increasing number of people across the world are reaping the benefits of the teachings of the Buddha. What is more, it is the fastest growing way of life in Europe and America today, the citadels of materialism and luxury. The rich and the famous, intellectuals, sportspersons, film stars, to cite a few broad examples, are embracing the teachings of the Buddha and are leading happy, healthy and peaceful lives.

The Geneva based International Coalition for the Advancement of Religious and Spirituality (ICARUS) has bestowed "The Best Religion in the World" award of 2009 on the Buddhist Community. The special award was voted on by an international round table of more than 200 religious leaders from every part of the spiritual specturm as they could find literally not one single instance of a war fought in the name of Buddhism.

To obtain the maximum benefit from the teachings of the Buddha, it is necessary to adopt them in our daily lives. It is the solemn duty of every believer to follow the *Dhamma* in its pristine purity and entirety. It is also the solemn duty of every follower to share the fruits of the *Dhamma* with others.

This book is a humble attempt at inspiring people to walk the path of the *Dhamma* easily and properly so that they can get the maximum advantage of this sublime philosophy of life and make their lives happier, healthier, and more peaceful, prosperous and meaningful.

Buddhist literature is the most voluminous and detailed literature in the world. It is like an ocean. The original words of the Buddha are contained in 82000 *suttas* and that of his chief disciples *Sariputta* and *Moggalan* which are treated of equal importance in another 2000 *suttas,* running into over fifteen thousand pages, are in the Pāli language. The commentaries on these original words are explained in thirty five thousand pages. Thus, the original Pāli literature itself is of fifty thousand pages. Yet, there are very few books, which briefly and meaningfully describe the life and the teachings of the Buddha, and the essence of the *Dhamma* in a simple language. Therefore, the main purpose of this book is to meet these twin objectives of inspiring the people and providing the essence of teachings of the Buddha in a concise form and keeping in mind the lay followers of the Buddha who want to begin their journey on the path of the *Dhamma.*

The book is divided into seven chapters. The first chapter contains a brief life history of the Buddha. As mentioned earlier in this note, there is a general, massive politico-economic progress across the world. However, the basic human instincts remain unchanged and uncivilised, which is the main cause of tension and unhappiness. This is apparent from the gruesome violent incidents taking place in various parts of the world and the atrocities on weaker sections of the society including children, women and the aged. Further, the exploitation of man by man is seen in every part of the world, and is increasing by the day. Such reptilian behaviour by man is one of the most shameful things that could happen in the 21st century. Therefore, the teachings of the Buddha that 'enmity is overcome by friendship, violence is overcome by peace and war does not solve any problem' are all the more relevant today. Whatever economic progress we may achieve, we cannot be happy unless we behave according to the laws of the nature, that is the *Dhamma*. The author is of the view that true happiness can happen only if we start walking on the path of the *Dhamma.* Keeping this in mind, the second chapter is devoted to the teachings of the Buddha, while the third chapter deals with the essence of the *Dhamma*.

Silā (morality), *Samādhi* (mastery over mind) and *Paññā* (wisdom) are the three main pillars of the *Dhamma* philosophy. They compliment, strengthen and reinforce each other. If any one of these pillars is weak, the other two also are bound to become weak. Considering the importance of this inter dependence, the fourth chapter is devoted to the law of cause and effect, while the fifth chapter is on *Vipassanā* meditation, India's most ancient meditation technique, in view of its importance vis-a-vis the three pillars. The Buddha taught *Vipassanā* and recognised its importance as a universal remedy for all the ills of mankind. *Vipassanā* enables purification of the mind by removing defilements such as craving, aversion and attachment. In a world filled with diversities of religion, language, beliefs and interests, it is the most effective practical path enabling one to live a life full of peace and happiness, without any animosity and conflict. *Vipassanā* is the practical, unifying and most quintessential tool for mental training to live a life in accordance with all religious teachings. It is the tool to directly experience the truth regarding the law of cause and effect: as the seed is so the fruit will be; as our action is, so will our happiness or suffering be. By selflessly serving others, we serve ourselves; by respecting other religions and communities we respect our own religion and community.

The Buddha also emphasised that there is no shortcut to the *Dhamma*. Every person has to work individually for one's salvation. No power in the universe can liberate one unless one works for it. Everyone is a master of one's own destiny. The Buddha has only shown the path of liberation; everyone seeking liberation from sufferings and miseries has to walk on that path himself/herself. There is no substitute for self-liberation.

The information given in this book has been taken from various books on the *Dhamma*. The author has freely used various publications of the *Vipassanā* Research Institute, Igatpuri. Tens of hundreds of volumes have been written about the Buddha and his teachings in the past 2,550 years. Keeping in view the contribution of various authors, I do not claim any originality for this book except for my own experience of the small journey on the path of the *Dhamma*. My effort has been to provide all the relevant information required by a lay follower at one place. However, for the readers who are interested in the vast ocean of *Pāli* literature, sixth chapter is devoted to Buddhist literature for those interested in the original works.

The Indian Subcontinent is the land of the Buddhas. The Buddhas in the past were infinite in number. From the available literature, the authors have documented 28 known Buddhas. Siddhāttha Gotama was the 28th Buddha. Buddhists believe that the 29th Buddha, the Maitreya Buddha, is yet to be born.

It is believed that the teachings of all Buddhas are the same as they always teach the *Dhamma* which is universal and eternal. However, wherever the word 'the Buddha' is referred to in the book, the reference is towards Gotama the Buddha.

I have tried to make every chapter self-contained. It is possible, therefore, that the readers may find some information overlapping. The Buddha taught the *Dhamma* in *Pāli* which was the common language of his time. The *Pāli* texts contain the original words of the Buddha. Sometimes it becomes difficult to convey the exact meaning in English. Therefore, in some places original *Pāli* words have been used in place of familiar English words. For example, Siddhāttha, which is the *Pāli* form, is used in place of the Sanskrit Siddhārtha and Gotama has been used in place of Sanskrit Gautama. Similarly, the original *Pāli* words like *Dhamma* in place of the Sanskrit *Dharma*, *Silā* instead of *Sheel*, *Paññā* instead of *Prajnā*, *Saṅkhāra* instead of *Saṁskāra* are used in this book. To make the text easier to understand, *Pāli* words have been pluralized in the English style by adding's'. I have kept *Pāli* words in the text to the minimum to maintain a smooth flow.

I have tried my level best to make the book error-free; still, to err is human. The esteemed readers are requested to point out any mistake and also offer valuable suggestions so that future editions of the book are improved accordingly.

I would like to admit that this is a very humble endeavour in the vast ocean of the *Dhamma,* and if I am able to ignite the flame of the *Dhamma* in my esteemed readers, I will have succeeded in my efforts.

I express my deep sense of gratitude to Principal Vipassanā Ācārya Pujya Guru Late Shri S. N. Goenkaji, who brought back *Vipassanā* meditation to India in 1969 and popularised it across the world with infinite love and compassion. I have gained a lot while walking on the path of the *Dhamma* under his guidance and blessings. This book is an expression of my gratitude to him.

I am also grateful to *Vipassanā* teacher Dr. R. M. Chokhani, Dr. Parihar and other *Dhamma* brothers of the *Vipassanā* Research Institute, Igatpuri, who not only helped me experience the *Dhamma* but also practise it. My discussions with them helped me remove the doubts and confusions I had about the *Dhamma*.

I also express my special thanks to Shri V. K. Baranwal and Col. Kamlesh Chandra for their valuable suggestions; and special thanks to brother Rajbhar Dinesh for giving me valuable suggestions and insights. I also thank my wife Dr. Manisha, daughter Pragya, son Rachit. My special thanks are due to Mr. Ravi Sethi & Mrs. Neeru Sethi, the entire team of Empty Canvas Publishers for taking up the responsibility of publication of this book.

ANAND S. KRISHNA
New Delhi

Chapter 1
Life of the Buddha

The Birth

Gotama, the Buddha, was born on a full moon day of Vesākha (April- May) in 563 BC[1] under a large Sala tree in the Lumbini Park near Kapilavatthu on the Indian borders of the present day Nepal. His childhood name was Siddhāttha Gotama (in Sanskrit Siddhārtha Gautama). Siddhāttha means 'wish fulfilled' and Gotama was his family name. His father was the king Suddhodana of the aristocratic Śākya clan and his mother was the queen Mahāmāyā.

Suddhodana was a great warrior and was therefore, allowed to have a second wife. He chose Mahāprajāpati, the sister of Mahāmāyā his first wife, as his second queen. Queen Mahāmāyā died seven days after giving birth to Gotama, following which Mahāprajāpati Gotami adopted the newborn child.

Ascetic Asita seeing the child Siddhatha

Asita the ascetic, who had high spiritual attainments, visited the palace to see the royal infant. On seeing the child, the ascetic rose from his seat and saluted him with folded hands as he foresaw the child's greatness. The great ascetic first expressed joy and then he shed tears profusely. When the king asked him about his reaction, he explained that he smiled because the prince would eventually become a Buddha, the Enlightened One, and teach the suffering humanity the way to eradicate misery. But he was sad because he would not be able to benefit by the supreme wisdom of the Enlightened One, as he would die before having that opportunity.

The Childhood

Siddhāttha was a quiet child who loved nature. Characteristically, he was loving, caring and compassionate towards all beings. His regular education started at the age of eight and he went to school with other children. He mastered whatever he was taught. Since his early childhood he was against the exploitation of any being.

Ploughing Festival

King Suddhodana owned a vast area of land. There used to be an annual ploughing festival marking the beginning of the sowing

Siddhāttha going to school

season and the king and the nobles participated in it to promote farming. When Siddhāttha was nine, he went to the fields to see the ploughing festival[2] accompanied by his friends. The function began with the chanting of the scriptures by the priests. It was so hot that Siddhāttha began to sweat in the blazing sun. He was shocked to see that the field labourers did not have enough clothes to protect them from the scorching heat. As the ploughs started furrowing the fields, the worms and other small creatures were killed in the process.

First Meditation

There was a rose-apple tree nearby. Siddhāttha left the function and took refuge in the shade of the tree. He sat under the tree with his legs crossed and spine erect. He closed his eyes and meditated with ease. He entered into the first *Jhāna*, a trance in which the meditating person feels calmness and happiness but can still think and reflect. He reflected on all that he had just seen and asked himself how it could be justified that the masters enjoy themselves at the cost of their servants? How can exploitation of labourers by landlords be justified? Why can't the recital of the scriptures relieve the poor farmers and labourers from their sufferings? Why can't it save the life of worms and insects?

First meditation under the roseapple tree

When the king Suddhodana saw his son meditating under the rose-apple tree, he was worried about the prophecy of the sage Asita coming true.

As a young prince, Siddhāttha had no interest in hunting. He used to tell his friends that he did not want to be a witness to the killing of innocent animals. His mother tried to persuade him to go for hunting on the plea that he was a *Kshatriya* and it was the duty of *Kshatriya*s to fight. In response, he asked her, "How can it be the duty of only one class of persons to fight? How can it be the duty of a man to fight and kill another man? Why can't all people live in peace? If the *Kshatriya*s love and respect each other why can't they protect their nation without fighting and killing each other?" To this she had no answer.

Siddhāttha studied literature, creative arts, athletics and archery with the other Śākya princes. He mastered many languages. He was not only an ace shooter but an excellent flutist as well. His teachers were always impressed by his talent and grasping power.

Marriage & Family Life

At the early age of sixteen, Siddhāttha was married to 'the beautiful and virtuous Yashodharā'[3] who was also of the same age. She was the daughter of the great Śākya Daṇḍapāni of the Koliya republic, who held an archery competition for eligible princes for his daughter to choose her husband. Siddhāttha stood first in the competition.

The king was happy to see his son married and leading family life. But the prophecy of the sage Asita continued to haunt him. To overcome the prophecy, he tried to keep Siddhāttha busy in mundane pleasures and carnal joys. He built three luxury palaces for his son – one for the summer, one for the rainy season and another for the winter – all furnished with the luxuries and excitements for an amorous life. A lake surrounded each palace, besides an extensive garden beautifully laid out with all kinds of flowers and trees. He also arranged for a harem with beautiful damsels to win over the prince. These beauties tried to entice the prince with every method known to them, but all of them failed.

Realising that the young women had failed to entice the prince, the king asked his Prime Minister Udāyin to persuade the prince to enjoy sensual pleasures. Udāyin tried his best but to no avail. Justifying the company of young women, Udāyin told Siddhāttha:

> Knowing that pleasure was the best of objects, even the god Purandara (Indra) wooed in olden times Ahalyā, the wife of the saint Gotama. So too Agastya wooed Rohini, the wife of Somā; and therefore, as Sruti saith, a like thing befell Lopamudrā. The great ascetic Brihaspati

> begot Bhāradvāja from Mamatā, the daughter of the Maruta, the wife of Autathya. So too in old times Parāsara, overpowered by passion on the banks of the Yamunā, laid with the maiden Kāli who was the daughter of the son of Varuṇā. And the seer- king Yayat, even when the vigour of his prime was gone, sported in the Kaitrartha forests with the Apsarā Visvaki. Great heroes such as these pursued even shameful desires for the sake of pleasure, how much more so when they are praiseworthy of their kind? And yet you, a young man who possesses strength and beauty, despise enjoyments which rightly belong to you and to which the whole world is devoted.[4]

Siddhāttha told the prime minister that he had no interest in sensual pleasures as they were impermanent. Explaining the lack of substance in sensual pleasures Siddhāttha said:

> I do not despise worldly objects. I know that all mankind is bound up therein. But remembering that the world is transitory, my mind cannot find pleasure in them. Yet, even if this beauty of women were to remain perpetual, still delight in the pleasures of desires will not be worthy for wise men. And as for what you said, as to even those great men having become victims to desire, do not be led away by them for destruction was also their lot. Real greatness is not to be found there, where there is destruction, or where there is attachment to earthly objects, or a want of self-control. And when you said, 'Let one deal with women by guile,' I know about guile, even if it were accompanied with courtesy. That compliance too with a woman's wishes pleases me not, if truthfulness be not there; if there be not a union with one's nature, then 'out upon it' I say. A man overpowered by passion, believing in falsehood, carried away by attachment and blind to the faults of its objects, what is there in it worth being deceived? And if the victims of passion do deceive one another, are not men unfit for women to look at and women for men? Since then these things are so, you surely would not lead me astray into ignoble pleasures.[5]

Udāyin fell silent by the firm resolve of the young prince. He reported the matter to the king. Being informed that the prince had no interest in sensual pleasures, the king could not sleep that night.

Siddhāttha used to stay in three different palaces alternatively depending upon the weather. Accompanied by his wife Yashodharā, he used to visit the people in the deep interiors and share their sorrows and pains. Soon he began to show keen interest in the administrative works of the kingdom, making his father happy and a bit relieved. Yet he tried to arrange all possible luxuries, including most beautiful dancers for the young prince. But Siddhāttha had no interest in them. What was more, the couple did not want to involve themselves in sensual pleasures. There was a perfect understanding between Siddhāttha and Yashodharā on this front. They had a lot of respect for each other and they continuously tried to find the solutions to the social problems they had seen in the villages and the spiritual questions which could help establish a new, just and egalitarian society.

Siddhāttha spent many months travelling through the length and breadth of his kingdom, understanding the problems of his subjects. He spent many nights in villages sharing his time with villagers. He ate with farmers, labourers, and village artisans and found them living in abject poverty. He met families who had as many as nine to ten children but could not feed them once a day. He saw people with sickness and with physical disabilities. And to make matters worse, the priests were exploiting them in the name of *Yagñas, havans* and *poojans*.

Siddhāttha realised that people were caught up in a vicious circle of poverty, exploitation, illness and suffering, which could not be solved without creating a new social system. But who will do it? He wondered. And how could it be possible? The poor villagers were not in a position to approach higher authorities, as the capital was far away. And even if they managed to do so, who would listen to them? Ministers and senior officers would not even meet them, leave alone solve their problems. He was aware that social problems and the selfishness and ambitions of politicians and officers were the root cause of various social, economic, political and militancy problems of his kingdom. They were so absorbed in their personal agenda that they had little time and interest for the welfare and progress of common people. They were always busy conspiring against each other to gain the confidence of the king so they could acquire the maximum power. They were busy in raising their status and eating, drinking and enjoying their own lives.

Do the authorities sitting in the capital have time to solve the problems of the poor and destitute? Can the prime minister solve their problems? Can the king solve their problems? These questions started pounding his mind, time and again. Siddhāttha realised that even the king was not in a position to bring fundamental changes in the social system. He knew that his officers were always busy in their personal agenda. This realisation created in him a sense of disillusionment towards politics. He realised that even the prime minister and the king were bound by the set norms and procedures, which took precedence over substance. The king was a slave of his own circumstances. This realisation made Siddhāttha disinterested in politics and statecraft. When he used to see the corrupt ministers and officers giving lectures on morality, honesty and virtues, his blood boiled with anger. But he had to keep quite as he had no effective and practical alternatives to offer.

One day his father asked him why he was not contributing his ideas in the court instead of sitting silently. Looking at his father, Siddhāttha replied: "It is not that I do not have ideas, but it would be useless to state them. They only point to a disease. I do not yet see a cure for the selfish ambitions of those in the court. Look at Vessamitta, for example. He holds an impressive amount of power in the court, yet you know he is corrupt. More than once he has tried to encroach upon your authority, but you are still forced to depend on his services because you know if you don't, chaos will break loose."[6]

Looking at Siddhāttha silently for a long time, his father spoke: "Siddhāttha, you know well that to maintain peace in one's family and the country, there are certain things one must tolerate. My own power is limited, but I am sure that if you prepared yourself to be the king, you would do far better than I have. You possess the talent needed to purge the ranks of corruption while preventing chaos in our homeland."[7]

Siddhāttha sighed: "Father, I do not think it is a question of talent. I believe the fundamental problem is to liberate one's own heart and mind. I too am trapped by the feelings of anger, jealousy, fear, and desire."[8]

Similar exchanges between the father and the son only increased the king's anxiety. He recognised that Siddhāttha was a person of unusual depth, and he saw how differently his son looked at the world. Still, he fostered the hope that over time, Siddhāttha would come to accept his role and fill it in the most worthy manner.

Thoughts like these relating to politics and spiritual life used to occupy Siddhāttha's mind. He was very well aware and alert about his duties. Therefore, when the time came, he subscribed to the membership of the *Śākya Saṅgha*.

Member of Śākya Saṅgha

The *Ś*ākyas were a democratic people. They had their *Saṅgha*. Every Śākyas youth above twenty had to be initiated into the *Saṅgha* and become a member. Siddhāttha was enrolled as a member when he turned twenty. The duties of a member of the *Saṅgha* were: safeguarding the interests of the Śākyas by body, mind and money; not abstaining from the meetings of the *Saṅgha*; exposing any fault in the conduct of a Śākya without fear or favour; and when accused, confess it if guilty, or offer explanation if innocent.

The conditions for disqualification of a member were: committing rape, murder, theft and giving false evidence.

Eight years passed since Siddhāttha was made a member of the Śākya *Saṅgha*. He was a very devoted and steadfast member. He took the same interest in the affairs of the *Saṅgha* as he did in his own. His conduct as a member was exemplary and he endeared himself to all.

Conflict with the Saṅgha

Bordering the kingdom of the Śākyas was the Koliya kingdom. The Rohini river divided the two. As both the Śākyas and the Koliyas used the Rohini waters for irrigating their fields, disputes existed between them as to who should take the water first and how much, etc, which often resulted in quarrels and sometimes even in wars. When Siddhāttha was twenty-eight, there was a major clash over the water issue between the two kingdoms and both sides suffered heavily. The Śākyas felt that the issue should be settled once and for all by waging a war. The commander of the Śākyas, therefore, called a session of the Śākya *Saṅgha* to consider the question of declaring a war on the Koliyas. Addressing the members of the *Saṅgha*, the commander said:

> Our people have been attacked by the Koliyas and they had to retreat. Such acts of aggression by the Koliyas have taken place more than once. We have tolerated them so far. But this cannot go on. It must be stopped and the only way to stop it is to declare war on them. I propose that the *Saṅgha* declare a war on the Koliyas. Those who wish to oppose may speak.[9]

Siddhāttha rose from his seat and said:

> I oppose this resolution. War does not solve any problem. Waging a war will not serve our purpose. It will sow the seeds of another war. The slayer gets a slayer in his turn; the conqueror gets one who conquers him; a man who despoils is despoiled in his turn. I feel that the *Saṅgha* should not be in a haste to declare war on the Koliyas. Careful investigation should be made to scertain who is the guilty party. I hear that our men have also been aggressors. If this is true, then it is obvious that we too are not free from blame.[10]

The commander replied: "Yes, our men were the aggressors. But it must not be forgotten that it was our turn to take the water first."[11]

Siddhāttha said: "This shows that we are not completely free from blame. I, therefore, propose that we elect two men from among us and the Koliyas should be asked to elect two from among them and the four should elect a fifth person and they should settle the dispute."

The amendment moved by Siddhāttha was duly seconded. But the commander opposed the amendment, saying: "I am sure that this menace of the Koliyas will not end unless they are severely punished." The resolution and the amendment were therefore put to vote. The amendment moved by Siddhāttha was put first. It was declared lost by an overwhelming majority. The commander then put his own resolution to vote. Siddhāttha again stood up to oppose it. "I beg the *Saṅgha*," he said, "not to accept the resolution. The *Śākyas* and the Koliyas are close relations. It is unwise that they should destroy each other."

The commander answered that it was the *Dharma* of the *Kshatriya*s to fight for the sake of their kingdom. Siddhāttha replied: "*Dharma*, as I understand it, consists of recognising that enmity does not disappear by enmity. It can be conquered by love only." The commander, getting impatient, said: "It is unnecessary to enter upon this philosophical disquisition. The point is that Siddhāttha is opposed to my resolution. Let's ascertain what the *Saṅgha* has to say about it by putting it to vote." Accordingly, the commander's resolution was put to vote. It was declared carried by an overwhelming majority.

Opposes War, Invites Exile

The next day, the commander convened another meeting of the *Saṅgha* to get his plan of mobilisation ratified by the *Saṅgha.* When the *Saṅgha* met, he told the gathering that he should be permitted to issue a conscription order for every Śākya between twenty and fifty to report to the army. Both sides — those who voted in favour of the war as well as those who voted against the war at the previous *Saṅgha* meeting — attended the meeting. While for those who voted in favour of the war there was no difficulty in accepting the proposal of the commander, the minority who voted against it had a problem — to submit or not to submit to the decision of the majority. The minority was determined not to submit to the majority. Unfortunately, none of them had the courage to do so openly. Seeing that his supporters were silent, Siddhāttha stood up, and addressed the *Saṅgha*:

> Friends! You may do what you like. You have a majority on your side, but I am sorry to say I shall oppose your decision in favour of mobilisation. I shall not join your army and I shall not take part in the war.[12]

This caused a tremendous stir. The commander told Siddhāttha: "Do remember the vows you had taken when you were admitted to the membership of the *Saṅgha*. If you break any of them you will expose yourself to public shame."

Siddhāttha replied: "Yes, I have pledged myself to safeguard the best interests of the Śākyas by my body, mind and money. But I do not think that this war is in the best interests of the Śākyas. What is public shame to me before the best interests of the Śākyas?"

Siddhāttha proceeded to caution the *Saṅgha* by reminding it of how the Śākyas had become the vassals of the Kosala king due to their quarrels with the Koliyas. "It is not difficult to imagine," he said, "that this war will give him a greater handle to further reduce the freedom of the Śākyas." The commander grew angry and told Siddhāttha: "Your eloquence will not help you. You must obey the majority decision. You are perhaps counting upon the fact that the *Saṅgha* has no power to order an offender to be hanged or to exile him without the sanction of the Kosala king and that the king will not give permission if either of the two sentences was passed against you by the *Saṅgha*. But remember that the *Saṅgha* has other ways of punishing you. The *Saṅgha* can declare a social boycott of your family and can confiscate your family's land. For this the *Saṅgha* does not have to obtain the permission of the Kosala king."

Siddhāttha realised the consequences that would follow if he continued his opposition to the war plans against the Koliyas. He had three alternatives to consider— to join the forces and participate in the war; to consent to being hanged or exiled; and to allow the members of his family to be condemned to a social boycott and confiscation of their property. He was firm in not accepting the first. As to the third, he felt it was unthinkable. Under the circumstances, he felt that the second alternative was the best. Accordingly, Siddhāttha told the *Saṅgha*. "Please do not punish my family. Do not put them in distress by subjecting them to a social boycott. Do not make them destitute by confiscating their land, which is their only means of livelihood. They are innocent. Let me alone suffer for my deeds. Sentence me to death or exile, whichever you like. I will willingly accept it and I promise I shall not appeal to the Kosala king."[13]

Parivraja — the Way Out

The commander said: "It is difficult to accept your suggestion. For even if you voluntarily agreed to undergo the sentence of death or exile, the matter is sure to become known to the Kosala king and he is sure to conclude that it is the *Saṅgha* which has inflicted this punishment and take action against the *Saṅgha*."

Siddhāttha said: "If this is the difficulty, I can easily suggest a way out. I can become a *Parivrājaka* and leave this country. It is a kind of exile."

The commander thought this was a good solution. But he had still some doubts about Siddhāttha being able to give effect to it. So, he asked Siddhāttha: "How can you become a *Parivrājaka* unless you obtain the consent of your parents and your wife?" Siddhāttha assured him that he would do his best to obtain their permission. "I promise," he said, "to leave this country immediately whether I obtain their consent or not." The *Saṅgha* felt that the proposal made by the prince was the best way out and they agreed. But when the meeting was about to be over, a young Śākya got up and said: "Give me a hearing, I have something important to say." After getting permission to proceed, he continued: "I have no doubt that Siddhāttha will keep his promise and leave the country immediately. There is, however, one question over which I do not feel very happy. Now that Siddhāttha will soon be out of sight, does the *Saṅgha* propose to give immediate effect to its declaration of war against the Koliyas? I want the *Saṅgha* to give further consideration to this question. In any event, the king of Kosala is bound to come to know of the exile of Siddhāttha. If the Śākyas declare a war against the Koliyas immediately, the king will understand that Siddhāttha left only because he was opposed to war. This will not go well with us. I, therefore, propose that we should also allow an interval to pass between the exile of Siddhāttha and the actual commencement of hostilities so as not to allow the king to establish any connection between the two."[14]

The *Saṅgha* realised that this was a very important proposal. As a matter of expediency, they accepted it. Thus ended the tragic session of the *Śākya Saṅgha* and the minority which was opposed to the war but who had no courage to say so, heaved a sigh of relief that it was able to overcome a situation full of calamitous consequences.

The Renunciation

The traditional view that Siddhāttha left home at night on seeing an old man, a sick man, a dead man and an ascetic, when his wife and other family members were sleeping, does not appear to be logical.

It is an accepted fact that when Siddhāttha abdicated his kingdom and palace, he was twenty-nine, that is, after thirteen years of his married life. He lost his mother when he was just seven days old. He was married at the age of sixteen. People of every age were present at his wedding. He used to take part in the annual ploughing festival along with many people of all ages. He was the member of a large royal family with a number of maids and servants. In such a large family somebody falling sick at one time or the other is not an unusual event. His father and stepmother were growing old in front of his eyes. As the royal family was very religious, ascetics regularly visiting them is not strange — the sage Asita visited the palace at the time of his birth. Hence there was no need for him to wait for twenty- nine years to realise this simple fact of life that people grow old, fall sick and one day die. Even little children ask us: why their grandmother or grandfather have grey hair or why have they grown old; why so and so has passed away; will we also die some day? If so, how is it possible that a man of Siddhāttha's intelligence would take so many years to realise these simple facts of life that people grow old, fall sick and die and that ascetics seek peaceful lives?

Prince Siddhāttha must have been moved by the realities of old age, sickness, death and the bliss of reclusive life and the impermanence of youth. When Siddhāttha grasped the realities of old age, disease and death, he was troubled–but not just because he himself would one day have to endure this suffering. The truth was that he developed immense compassion for the countless beings who suffer these miseries. Then the question arose in his mind: is there a way out of this misery for all beings? He was confident that :

where so many miseries exist, there also exists (ultimate) happiness;

where (repeated) births exist, there also exists the desired state of no birth;

for those encumbered by afflictions due to past deeds, there is a noble path of deliverance;

He used to contemplate that if there was birth, aging, illness, death, sorrow and corruption in our lives, there must be positive counterparts as well; there must be another mode of existence and, therefore, it was up to him to find it out. He wanted to find out that path which gives liberation from the cycle of becoming.

The Buddha has often been criticised for leaving behind his beautiful young wife and newly-born son and his tearful parents. The critics forget that Siddhāttha, after attaining Enlightenment, helped them attain the infinite happiness of Liberation. If he had remained at home, he would have been able to give them only the lesser happiness of worldly comforts and companionship. Instead, his entire family attained complete Liberation[15].

Some also criticise him on the ground that he left home in search of the truth and not with the intention of helping others. In other words, they allege that Siddhāttha chose homelessness only to satisfy his curiosity or to serve himself. But these critics ignore the fact that Siddhāttha was a *Bodhisatta*. He did not discover the path of Liberation only for himself, he did it to help all human beings. It is only after attaining perfect Enlightenment that he could help all beings to liberate themselves. Without liberating himself first from the defilements of craving and aversion, he could not have shown the path of complete Liberation to others. It would have been a case of a blind man leading another blind man. Though conflict with the *Śākya Saṅgha* precipitated Siddhāttha's self- renunciation, his main objective of leaving material life was not just to fulfil his curiosity about the ultimate truth, but to liberate himself and also to help others. Therefore, it is 'incorrect and most unfortunate to say that the Buddha chose the life of homelessness to serve himself' [16] or that he left home in the wee hours when his wife and other family members were sleeping.

The Truth about Renunciation

The truth is that Siddhāttha renounced worldly life with the consent of his family and in their full knowledge. Siddhāttha's conversation with his family members is worth reading:[16a]

Parting Words

Suddhodana: We were talking about the evils of war. But I never thought that you would go to such lengths.

Siddhãttha: I too did not think things would take such a turn. I was hoping that I would be able to win over the *Śākyas* to the cause of peace by my argument. Unfortunately, our military officers had so worked up the feelings of the men that my argument failed to have any effect on them. But I hope you realise how I have saved the situation from becoming worse. I have not given up the cause of truth and justice and whatever the punishment for my standing for truth and justice; I have succeeded in making its infliction personal to me.

Suddhodana: You have not considered what will happen to us.

Siddhãttha: But that is the reason why I undertook to become a *Parivrājaka*. Consider the consequences if the Śākyas ordered the confiscation of your lands.

Suddhodana: But without you what is the use of these lands to us? Why should not the whole family leave the country of the Śākyas and go into exile along with you?

Prajāpati Gotami: I agree. How can you go alone leaving us here like this?

Siddhãttha: Mother, have you not always claimed to be the mother of a *Kshatriya*? Is that not so? You must then be brave. This grief is unbecoming of you. What would you have done if I had gone to the battlefield and died? Would you have grieved like this?

Gotami: No. That would have been befitting a *Kshatriya*. But you are now going into the jungles far away from people, living in the company of wild beasts. How can we stay here in peace? I say you should take us along with you.

Siddhãttha: How can I take you all with me? Nanda, my cousin, is only a child. Rāhula, my son, is just born. Can you come leaving them here?

Gotami: It is possible for us all to leave the country of the

Śākyas and go to the country of the Kosala under the protection of their king.

Siddhãttha: But, mother, what would the Śākyas say? Would

they not regard it as treason? Besides, I pledged that I would do nothing either by word or by deed to let the king of the Kosala know the true cause of my *Prabrajyā*. It is true that I may have to live alone in the forest. But which is better? To live in the forest or to be a party to the killing of the Koliyas!

Suddhodana: But why this impatience? The Śākya *Saṅgha* has decided to postpone the date of the hostilities for some time. Perhaps the hostilities may not be started at all. Why not postpone your *Prabrajyā?* Maybe it would be possible to obtain the permission of the *Saṅgha* for you to stay among the Śākyas.

Siddhāttha: It is because I promised to take *Prabrajyā* that the *Saṅgha* decided to postpone the commencement of hostilities against the Koliyas. It is possible that after I take *Prabrajyā* the *Saṅgha* may be persuaded to withdraw the declaration of war. All this depends upon my first taking *Prabrajyā*. I have made a promise and I must carry it out. The consequences of any breach of promise may be very grave both to us and to the cause of peace. Mother, do not now stand in my way. Give me your permission and your blessings. What is happening is for the best."

Gotami and Suddhodana kept silent.

Then Siddhāttha went to the apartment of Yashodharā. Seeing her, he stood silent, not knowing what to say and how to say it. Yashodharā broke the silence:

Yasodharā: I have heard all that has happened at the meeting of the *Saṅgha* at Kapilavatthu.

Siddhāttha: Yasodharā, tell me what do you think of my decision to take *Prabrajyā*?

Yashodharā: What else could I have done if I were in your position? I certainly would not have been a party to a war on the Koliyas. Your decision is the right decision. You have my consent and my support. I too would have taken *Prabrajyā* with you. If I do not, it is only because I have Rāhula to look after. I wish it had not come to this. But we must be bold and brave and face the situation. Do not be anxious about your parents and your son. I will look after them till there is life in me. All I wish is that now that you are becoming a *Parivrājaka* leaving behind all who are near and dear to you, you will find a new way of life which would result in the happiness of mankind."

Siddhāttha asked Yasodharā to bring Rāhula. Casting his fatherly eyes on his little son, he took the final bow and left.

The Great Renunciation

Siddhāttha thought of taking *Prabrajyā* at the hands of Bharadwāja who had his āshrama at Kapilavatthu. Accordingly, he got up the next day and started off for the āshrama on his favourite horse Kanthaka with his servant Channa walking along. As he came nearer to the āshrama, men and women came out and thronged the gates to meet him. With great difficulty he extricated himself from the crowd and entered the gates of the ashrama. His father Suddhodana and mother Prajāpati Gotami were also present there to witness his *Prabrajyā*. Siddhāttha went to the place where Channa was standing. He gave him his dress and ornaments to take back home. Then he had his head shaved, as was required for a *Parivrājaka*. His cousin Mahānāma had brought the clothes and an alms bowl appropriate for a *Parivrājaka*. Siddhāttha wore them. Having thus prepared himself to enter the life of a *Parivrājaka*, Siddhāttha approached Bharadwāja to confer on him the required *Prabrajyā.* Bharadwāja, with the help of his disciples, performed the necessary ceremonies and declared Siddhāttha Gotama to have become a *Parivrājaka*. Remembering that he gave a double pledge to the Śākya *Saṅgha* to take *Prabrajyā* and to leave the

Siddhattha leaving home

Śākya kingdom without any undue delay, immediately after the ceremony, Siddhāttha started off his journey. As the prince stepped out of the *āshrama* the waiting crowd also followed him. He left Kapilavatthu and proceeded in the direction of the river Anomā. Looking back he saw the crowd still following him. He stopped and addressed them:

> Brothers and sisters, there is no use in following me. I could not settle the dispute between the Śākyas and the Koliyas. But if you create public opinion in favour of a settlement you might succeed. Be, therefore, so good as to return.[17]

Hearing his appeal, the crowd started to go back. Suddhodana and Gotami also returned to the palace. People admired him and sighed for him saying: "Here was a Śākya blessed with high lineage, noble parentage, possessed of considerable riches, in the bloom of youthful vigour, accomplished in mind and body, brought up in luxury, who fought his kinsmen for the sake of maintaining peace on the earth and goodwill towards men. Here is a Śākya youth who when outvoted by his kinsmen refused to submit, but preferred to undergo voluntary punishment which involved the exchange of riches for poverty, comfort for alms, home for homelessness. And so he goes with none in the world to care for him and with nothing in the world, which he could claim as his own. His is an act of supreme sacrifice willingly made. His is a brave and a courageous act. There is no parallel to it in the entire history of the world. He deserves to be called a Śākya Muni or Śākya Singh."[18]

How true were the words of Kisā Gotami, a Śākya maiden, when referring to Siddhāttha, she said: "Blessed indeed is the mother, and blessed indeed is the father to have such a son. Blessed indeed is the wife who has such a husband."[19]

Channa refused to go back to the palace. He insisted on seeing the prince off with Kanthaka to the banks of the Anomā. On reaching the banks, Siddhāttha told Channa:

> I am pleased with your noble feelings towards me, even though I am powerless to confer any reward. People commonly become mere strangers in a reverse of fortunes. A son is brought up for the sake of the family, the father is honoured by the son for the sake of his own

> future support; the world shows kindness for the sake of hope; there is no such thing as unselfishness without a motive. But you are an exception. Take now this horse and return. Tell my father I have left him – with no thirst for heaven, with no lack of love, nor feeling of anger. Try to convince him that union, however long it may last, in time will come to an end. Since separation is certain, how shall there not be repeated severing from one's kindred? At a man's death there are doubtless heirs to his wealth but heirs to his merit are hard to find on the earth or exist not at all. The king, my father, requires to be looked after. The king may say, 'He is gone at a wrong time' But there is no wrong time for duty.

Change is inevitable in corporeal beings who are subject to different births. Even if I, through affection, were not to abandon my kindred, death would still make us helplessly abandon one another. As birds go to their roosting tree and then depart, so the meeting of beings inevitably ends in separation."

Seeing his horse Kanthaka in tears, Gotama stroked him with his hands and addressed him like a friend: *"Shed not tears, Kanthaka, bear with it, thy labours will soon have its fruit."*[20]

Hearing these words, Channa left with Kanthaka for Kapilavatthu.

The Journey to Rājagraha

Leaving Kapilavatthu, Siddhāttha proceeded to Rājagraha, ruled by the king Bimbisāra. Rājagraha was the seat of great philosophers and thinkers. On his way he visited Saki, Padma and the sage Raivata. All of them entertained him.

After a long and arduous journey of nearly four hundred miles by foot, Siddhāttha reached Rājagraha and made a small hut at the foot of the Pāṇḍava Hills.

Bimbisāra Persuades Siddhāttha

Next day, Siddhāttha went into the city with an alms bowl asking for alms. A vast crowd gathered around him. On hearing the news, the king Bimbisāra asked his courtier to follow him to find out his whereabouts.

On being informed by the royal courtier, the king ascended the hill to meet Siddhāttha. Bimbisāra advised him to give up the mendicant's life.

The king told Siddhāttha: "I am ready to give you one half of my kingdom. Pursue according to the rules of religious merit, wealth, and pleasure; pursue love and rest, in reverse order. These are the three objects in life; when men die they pass into dissolution as regards this world. By pursuing the three objects of life, your personality will bear its fruits; they say that when the attainment of religion, wealth and pleasure is complete in all its parts, then the end of a man is complete. Your two arms are worthy to conquer the three worlds, what to speak of the earth. I speak this to you out of affection — I am filled with compassion and I shed tears. O, who desires the mendicant's stage of life? Enjoy the pleasures now, in due time old age comes on and overcomes this beauty, well worthy of your illustrious race. Or if religion is really your aim, then offer sacrifices — this is your family's immemorial custom, climbing to the highest heaven by sacrifices. Royal sages have reached the same goal by sacrifice which great sages reached by self-mortification." [21]

Siddhāttha's reply to the king was that he was not interested in transient pleasures. He told the king that he had not renounced his home due to anger or defeat or fear or any desire for the heavens. He said:

> I have not left home through anger, nor because my diadem has been dashed down by an enemy's arrow; nor have I set my desires on loftier objects, that I thus refuse thy proposal. I have been wounded by the strife of the world, and I have come out longing to obtain peace; I would not accept any empire.
>
> But as for what you said to me, O King, that the universal pursuit of the three objects is the supreme end of man and you say that what I regard as the desirable is misery– your three objects are perishable and also unsatisfying.
>
> And as for what you said, 'wait till old age comes, for youth is ever subject to change', this want of decision

is itself uncertain; for age too can be irresolute and youth can be firm.

But since Fate is so well skilled in its art as to draw the world in all its various ages into its power, how shall the wise man, who desires tranquillity, wait for old age, when he knows not when the time of death will be?

When death stands ready like a hunter, with old age as his weapon, and diseases scattered about as his arrows, smiting down living creatures who fly like deer to the forest of destiny, what desire can there be in anyone for length of life?

It well befits the youthful son or the old man or the child so to act with all promptitude that they may choose the path of the religious man whose soul is all mercy. I have been wounded by the strife of the world, and I have come out longing to obtain peace;

And as for what you said, be diligent in sacrifices for religion, such as are worthy of your race and bring a glorious fruit, honour to such sacrifices! I desire not that fruit that is sought by causing pain to others! To kill a helpless victim through a wish for future reward

—it would be unseemly action for a merciful, good-hearted man, even if the reward of the sacrifice were eternal. And even if true religion did not consist of quite another rule of conduct, by self-restraint, moral practice and a total absence of passion, still it would not be seemly to follow the rule of sacrifice, where the highest reward is described as attained only by slaughter. Even that happiness which comes to a man, while he stays in this world, through the injury of another, is hateful to the wise compassionate heart; how much more if it be something beyond our sight in another life?

I am not to be lured into a course of action for future reward, my mind does not delight, O King, in future births; these actions are uncertain and wavering in their direction, like plants beaten by the rain from a cloud.[22]

The king realised the firmness of Siddhāttha's decision. He wished him success and requested him to come back to his kingdom as soon as he succeeded in his goal. Siddhāttha promised to visit him. The king returned to the palace.

News of Peace

While Siddhāttha was staying in Rājagraha five other *Parivrajaka-s* joined him and put up their huts by the side of his hut. These five *Parivrājaka-s* were Koṇḍañña, Assaji, Vappa, Mahānāma and Bhaddiya. They questioned him over the issue in the same way, as did the king Bimbisāra. When he explained to them the circumstances that led him to take exile, they said: "We have heard of it. But do you know what has happened since you left?"

Siddhāttha replied that he had no idea. Then they told him that after he left Kapilavatthu there was a great agitation among the Śākyas against going to war with the Koliyas. There were demonstrations and processions by men and women, boys and girls, carrying flags with such slogans as 'Koliyas are our brothers, it is wrong for a brother to fight against brother;' 'Think of the exile of Siddhāttha' and so on. The result of the agitation was that the Śākya *Saṅgha* had to convene a meeting and reconsider the question. This time the majority was for compromise with the Koliyas. The *Saṅgha* decided to select five Śākyas to act as their envoys and negotiate peace with the Koliyas. When the Koliyas heard of this they were very glad. They too selected five Koliyas to deal with the Śākya envoys. The envoys from the two sides met and agreed to appoint a permanent council of arbitration with the authority to settle every dispute regarding the sharing of the Rohini waters and both the sides agreed to abide by its decision. Thus the threatened war ended in peace.

After informing Siddhāttha of what had happened at Kapilavatthu, the *Parivrājaka-s* said, "There is now no need for you to continue to be a *Parivrājaka*. Why don't you go home and join your family?"

Siddhāttha said: "I am happy to hear this good news. It is a triumph for me. But I will not go back home. I must not. I must continue to be a *Parivrājaka*."

Siddhāttha asked the five *Parivrājaka-s* about their programme. They replied, "We have decided to do *Tapasyā*. Why don't you join us?" Siddhāttha said, "I must examine other ways first." The five *Parivrājaka-s* then left.

In Search of the Root of Conflicts

The news brought by the five *Parivrājaka-s* that the Koliyas and Śākya-s had made peace, made Siddhāttha review the entire development. Left alone, he began to reflect on his own position and to make sure if any reason was left for him to continue his *Prabrajyā*. He left his home because he opposed the war. 'Now that the war did not take place, is there any problem left for me? Does my problem end because a battle has not been waged?' he asked himself. On deep reflection, he realised that the problem of war is essentially a problem of conflict. It is only part of a larger problem. This conflict is going on not only between kings and nations but also between nobles and Brahmins, between householders, between mother and son, between son and mother, between father and son, between sister and brother, between companions. The conflict between nations is occasional but the conflict between classes is constant and perpetual. It is this, which is the root of all sorrows and sufferings in the world. 'True, I left home on account of war. But I cannot go back home although the war between the Śākyas and Koliyas was not waged. Now I see that my problem has become wider. I have to find a solution for this problem of social conflicts. '[23]

How far do the old-established philosophies offer a solution of this problem? Could he accept any of the social philosophies? He decided to examine everything for himself.

Halts at Bhrigu's Āshrama

With the intention of pursuing other ways, Siddhāttha left Rājagraha to meet Ālāra Kālāma. On his way he visited the hermitage of Bhrigu. He saw the inmates of the *āshrama* doing strange penances. Then Bhrigu explained to Siddhāttha all kinds of penances and the fruits thereof. 'Uncooked food, vegetables grown in ponds, roots and fruits– this is the food of the saints according to the sacred texts; but the different alternatives of penance vary. Some live like the birds on gleaned corn; others graze on grass like the deer; others live in the air like the snakes as if turned into anthills; others win their nourishment with great efforts from stones; others eat corn ground with their own teeth; some, having boiled for others, keep for themselves what may chance to be left; others with their tufts of matted hair continually wet with water, twice offer oblations to Agni with hymns; others, plunging like fishes into the water, dwell there with their bodies scratched by tortoises. By such penances endured for a time by the higher.... they attain heaven, by the lower the world of men, by the path of pain they eventually dwell in happiness, pain, they say, is the root of merit.'[23a]

Their devotion was for the sake of heaven. But Siddhāttha was interested in finding solution to the ills of life on earth. So, he thanked the company of sages and departed. Leaving the *āshrama* of Bhrigu, Siddhāttha went to the *āshrama* of Ālāra Kālāma at Vesālī to learn *Samādhi Mārga.*

Practice of Samādhi Marga

At that time there were three schools of the *Dhyāna Mārga* (meditation). All of them had one thing in common—control of breathing is the means of achieving *Dhyāna*. One school followed a way of breath observation called *Ānāpānasati;* another school followed the way of breath control called *Prāṇayāma,* while the third was the *Samādhi* School.

Ālāra Kālāma was well known as the master of *Dhyāna Mārga*. It consisted of seven stages. Siddhāttha learned the technique of all the seven stages from Ālāra Kālāma. He realized the meditative state called "*the realm of limitless space,*" in which the mind becomes one with the infinity, all material and visual phenomenon cease to arise, and space is seen as the limitless source of all things. But this did not liberate him from his deepest anxieties and sorrows. He further practiced the next stage of meditation and realized the realm of limitless consciousness in which he saw that his own mind was present in every phenomenon in the universe. But even this could not liberate him from his deepest afflictions and anxieties. Thereafter, he meditated to realize the next stage, *"the realm of no materiality"* – a state in which the meditator see that no phenomenon exists outside of his own mind. Within a month he attained the state of *"the realm of no materiality"*.

But even this state could not dissolve the deepest obstructions in his mind and heart. Knowing the meditative achievements of Siddhāttha, Ālāra Kālāma said, "Siddhāttha, you are profoundly gifted. You have attained the highest level I can teach. All I have attained, you have attained as well. Let us join together to guide and lead this community of monks.[24]

Siddhāttha was silent as he contemplated Ālāra Kālāma's invitation. While *"the realm of no materiality"* was a precious fruit of meditation, it did not help resolve the fundamental problem of birth and death, nor did it liberate one from all suffering and anxiety. It did not lead to total Liberation. Siddhāttha's goal was not to become the leader of a community, but to find the path of true Liberation. Therefore, he politely refused the invitation and left the *āshrama*. From there he went to the *āshrama* of Uddaka Rāmaputta near Rājagraha. Ācārya Uddaka was seventy five years old and was venerated by all for his spiritual achievements. When Siddhāttha explained to him that he had already attained *"the realm of no materiality"*, Uddaka was impressed and saw in him potential of becoming his spiritual heir. He taught him *"the state of neither perception nor non perception"*, a stage of meditative consciousness in which both perception and non-perception are eliminated. Siddhāttha attained it within two weeks. He realized that "*the state of neither perception nor non-perception"* allowed him to transcend all ordinary states of consciousness. But it did not solve the problem of life and death. It was not helping in final liberation from the sufferings of life. When Siddhāttha told Ācārya Uddaka about his attainment of *"the state of neither perception nor non-perception"*. Uddaka said, "You have attained the highest level I have. I am old and not long for this world. If you will remain here, we can guide this community together and when I die you can take my place as the master of the community."[25] But Siddhāttha declined the offer as he knew that *"the state of neither perception nor non-perception"* was not the key to liberation from the cycle of birth and death and, therefore, he left the *āshrama*.

Despite learning the seven *Jhānas* from Ālāra Kālāma and the eighth *Jhānas* from Uddaka Rāmaputta, Siddhāttha was not satisfied. Although his mind was calm and peaceful and purified to a great extent, still at the deepest level of his unconscious mind, there remained latent defilements. His mind was still not totally free. Therefore, Siddhāttha went to the Magadha country to learn the technique of *Dhyāna Mārga*, based on controlling breathing which was different from what was being practised in the Kosala country. The technique was not to breathe but to attain concentration by stopping breathing. Siddhāttha mastered this technique as well. When he tried concentration by stopping breathing he felt a piercing sound in his ears, and a feeling of his head being pierced by a sharp pointed knife. It was a very painful process. However, its practice did not solve the basic problem of suffering. Therefore, Siddhāttha rejected the *Samādhi Marga* also. In this way Siddhāttha tried all the known techniques of that time by roaming from one *āshrama* to another for about five years. But no one could answer the basic questions of life and death to his satisfaction and no one could show him the path of complete Liberation. Not satisfied with any of the known methods of meditation, he proceeded to try asceticism.

Practice of Asceticism

Siddhāttha proceeded to Uruvela, near the town of Gayā, to practise asceticism. He went up the Dangsiri (Dungeshwari) mountains, about six-and-a-half kilometres off Bodh Gayā. It was a lonely, solitary place on the banks of the river Nerañjarā. There he again met the five *Parivrājakas* whom he met at Rājagraha, while practising asceticism. The mendicants approached Siddhāttha and requested him to take them along with him and he agreed to do so.

The austerities and self-mortification practiced by Siddhāttha were the severest. Sometimes he visited only one house for alms. Sometimes he took only seven morsels. He fasted for days together. The five monks found it impossible to keep up with him. Later on he stopped bathing and even taking his share of food.

He lived to torment and torture his body. Dirt and filth accumulated on his body for years and began to automatically drop off. He took up his abode in the depths of the forest, which was so awesome that it was said that none but the senseless could venture to go in. When the winters brought chilly nights, he sat meditating in the open air, day in and day out. He lived on a single grain or a single fruit a day; and his body began to grow emaciated in the extreme. If he sought to feel his belly, it was his backbone that he found in his grasp; if he sought to feel his backbone he found himself grasping his belly, so closely had his belly caved in to his backbone. His body began to look nothing more than loose flesh hanging on protruding bones. He did not cut his hair or beard for six months, and when he rubbed his head, handfuls of hair fell off as though there was no longer any space for them to grow on the bit of flesh still clinging to his skull.

Abandons Asceticism

Siddhāttha's severe austerities and mortification lasted for six months. At the end of the sixth month, his body became so weak that he was unable to move. Yet, he was away from his objective — solving the problem of the manifold miseries in the world.

He told himself, "This is not the way to perfect Liberation."

And then one day, while practicing sitting-meditation in a cemetery, Siddhāttha with a jolt realised how wrong his path of self-mortification was. The sun was set and a cool breeze gently caressed his skin. After sitting all day beneath the blazing sun, the breeze was delightfully refreshing, and Siddhāttha experienced a mental ease that was completely unlike anything he felt during the day. He realised that body and mind formed one reality that could not be separated. The peace and comfort of the body was directly related to the peace and comfort of the mind. To abuse the body was to abuse the mind. Can the mortification of the body be called *Dhamma*? Siddhāttha realised that it was only by the authority of the mind that the body either acted or ceased to act, therefore, to control the thought was alone befitting — without thought the body was like a dog. Liberation could not be attained by him who had lost his strength and was weary with hunger, thirst and fatigue. The problems of human life could be found in the human body itself. The problem of fear, worry, dissatisfaction, hatred, jealousy and suffering all happen in the human body. Therefore, the solution to the problems is also to be found in the human body itself. The human body is the proportional composition of mind, mental concomitant and body. The mind and mental concomitant are not only the origin of the problems of human beings; the solutions to these problems have also to be found in them. He realised that true calm and self-possession of the mind were properly obtained by constantly satisfying the needs of the body.

Therefore, he decided to give up the practice of asceticism and resolved to regain his health and to use meditation to nourish both his body and the mind. From the next morning onwards, he started his alms rounds again. He decided that henceforth he would be "his own teacher" and not depend on the teachings of anyone else, and that he would discover his own path of liberation on his own. Having decided to give up asceticism, Siddhāttha accepted the offering of rice pudding from Sujātā.

Sujātā was the daughter of a householder named Senānī of Uruvela. She had uttered a wish to a pipal tree. To fulfil her wish, she sent out her maid Puṇṇā to prepare the place for the offering. On finding Siddhāttha sitting beneath the pipal tree, Puṇṇā thought he was the god of the tree who had come down. Sujātā came and

Sujātā offering rice pudding to Siddhāttha

offered him the food prepared in a bowl. He took the bowl to the river, bathed at a bathing place called Suppatitthita and ate the food. With this ended his practice of asceticism.

The five ascetics who were with Siddhāttha became angry

with him for giving up the life of austerity and self-mortification and they left him. Siddhāttha reflected upon his achievements of the last five-and-a-half years, and realised that all the paths had failed him. The failure was so complete that it could have led anyone into frustration. He was, of course, sorry. But frustration as such did not touch him. He was always hopeful of finding a way. He recollected the meditation that he did under a rose-apple tree during the ploughing festival when he was a nine-year-old boy. Soon, Siddhāttha started taking regular food once a day to recover his health. Sometimes he used to go out for alms to nearby villages and sometimes he used to accept the food brought by Sujātā. In this way, he nourished his body for some time.

Enlightenment is a slow process. It cannot be achieved suddenly. "Just as the ocean slopes, fall away gradually, and shelves gradually with no sudden incline," the Buddha later advised his disciples, "so, in this method, training, discipline and practice take effect by slow degrees, with no sudden perception of the ultimate truth."[26]

Meditation for Enlightenment

Siddhāttha used to take food in the forenoon and meditate for the rest of the time. He meditated on his body, on his feelings, on his perceptions, on his thoughts, on the interactions between body and mind and also on the way the universe works. He practiced mindfulness and developed great powers of concentration. Every-day in meditation he would practice *Metta Bhāvanā* (the meditation of loving kindness – "that huge, expansive and immeasurable feeling that knows no hatred")[26A] towards all beings. He would practice the four *Jhānas*. First, he cultivated a feeling of friendship for all beings. In the second *Jhānas* he cultivated compassion. In the third *Jhānas* he cultivated *Mudita* or sympathetic joy that rejoices at the happiness of others. In the last *Jhānas* he cultivated total equanimity (not reacting to pleasant and unpleasant sensations). In this way Siddhāttha meditated for six months. While in deep meditation, he started discerning the presence of countless other beings in his own body at the same time. On the full moon day of Vesākha in 528 BC, he thought of sitting under a *Pipala* tree in meditation, in the hope of a new light dawning upon him and enabling him to find a way that would solve all his problems. After trying each of the four directions he had chosen the east, the region of the dawn, which has always been chosen by all great sages to remove all defilements. Siddhāttha sat down cross- legged and upright under the *Pipala* tree. It is said that the pipal tree emits oxygen during the night also.

Mara's attack and temptation

Enlightenment

On the full moon day of the month of *Vesākha* (April-May), after having refreshed himself in the Nerañjarā river, Siddhāttha arrived at an inviting grove of trees. There he sat down under a pipal tree with a determination (*Adhitthana*) not to leave his seat before attaining Enlightenment. "Let my skin and sinews and bones dry up, together with all the flesh and blood of my body! I will welcome it! But I will not move from this spot until I have attained the supreme and final wisdom."[27]

As he sat down for meditation a crowd of evil thoughts and evil passions, all the unconscious elements within the psyche, which fight against our liberation (mythically called the children of Māra), entered his mind. Siddhāttha was greatly worried lest they should overpower him and defeat his purpose. He knew that in this battle with evil passions many sages had succumbed. So he summoned all the courage he had and told Māra, "Faith is found in me, and heroism and wisdom. How can ye evil passions defeat me? The streams even of rivers may this wind dry up. Ye would be unable to dry up my resolutions, when I am so intent. Better to me is death in battle than that I should be defeated in life."[28]

Seeing the firmness and strong determination of Siddhāttha, all the evil passions and negative thoughts (Māra) disappeared. He spent that night in deep meditation and discovered the technique of *Vipassanā*. While practising *Vipassanā* meditation, he realised that there were two problems. The first problem was that there was suffering in the world: every human being is suffering due to one reason or the other. The second problem was how to remove this suffering and make the mankind happy. By analysing and dividing his body and mind to the smallest part of the atom, he found that the body was made up of '*Asṭakalāpas'* (four basic elements of earth, fire, water and wind along with their characteristics). These *Asṭakalāpas* are continuously arising and passing away with such a great speed that though the body mass looks constant, the fact is that every moment the old body dies and a new body is born. The entire mass of body and mind is in a continuous flux and continuous flow. There is nothing but a mass of vibrations. Due to ignorance, the mind is reacting to the pleasant and unpleasant sensations generated on the body.

The mind develops craving for pleasant sensations and aversion against unpleasant sensations. These cravings and aversions result in the production of *Saṅkhāra-s (reactions),* which defile purity of the mind. If the stock of defilements in the form of *Saṅkhāra-s* of craving and aversion is more, so will be the suffering. The lesser the stock of *Saṅkhāra-s,* lesser the suffering. Due to ignorance, we keep on generating *Saṅkhāra- s* every moment. These *Saṅkhāra-s* lead to *Taṇhā* (craving). *Taṇhā* (craving) leads to becoming, which in turn leads to birth. Whenever, there is birth, mind and matter will combine and the six sensory organs will accompany, which will result in suffering due to old age, decay, death, union with unpleasant and parting with the pleasant. When the mind stops reacting to the pleasant and unpleasant sensations generated in the body, no more new *Saṅkhāra-s* will be generated. The habit pattern of the mind is such that when the generation of new *Saṅkhāra-s* is stopped, the old stock of accumulated *Saṅkhāra-s* starts coming on the surface of mind and getting evaporated. By this process when the entire stock of *Saṅkhāra-s* gets evaporated and generation of new *Saṅkhāra-s* is stopped, the mind becomes pure from defilements. With the realisation of *Anicca* (impermanence), the *Paññā* (direct experiential wisdom) is developed. To develop *Paññā, Samādhi* (concentration of mind) is a must. To get established in *Samādhi,* practice of five precepts — *Sīla* (morality) is must. *Vipassanā* meditation penetrates the veils of ignorance, delusion and illusion, which in turn leads to the experience of the ultimate truth in all its purity.

Through *Vipassanā* meditation, Siddhāttha penetrated the illusion of a solid mind and body, dissolved the tendency of his mind to cling and crave, realised the unconditional truth, and discovered the Law of Dependent Origination (*Paṭicca samuppāda*) and the chain of cause and effect conditioning the universe. Further, he realised by his own direct experience that

The Enlightement, Sanchi

whatever arises through a cause can cease, and by eliminating the causes that make one suffer, one can attain real happiness and liberation from all the miseries. He discovered the Four Noble Truths and a noble Eightfold Path. With this the darkness of ignorance was dispelled in him, and the light of wisdom shone forth in all its brilliance. The subtlest defilements of his mind were washed away. All the shackles were broken. No cravings remained in him for the future; his mind became free from all attachments. He discovered a new path. *Bodhisatta* Siddhāttha Gotama attained supreme Enlightenment and became a *Sammāsambuddha.* With the taste of supreme liberation, the following words of ecstasy (*Udana*) came forth:

Anekajāti saṁṣāraṁ sandhāvissaṁ anibbisaṁ,
Gahakārakaṁ gavesanto dukkhā jāti punappunaṁ.
Gahakāraka diṭṭho' si puna gehaṁ na kāhasi,
Sabbā te phāsukā bhaggā gahakūṭaṁ visaṅkhitaṁ,
Visaṅkhāragataṁ cittaṁ taṇhānaṁ khayaṁ'ajjhagā.

(Through many a birth I wandered in *Saṁsāra*, seeking, but not finding, the builder of the house. I have been taking birth in misery again and again. O builder of the house, you are now seen! You cannot build the house again. All the rafters and the central pole are shattered. The mind is free from all the *Saṅkhāra*. The stage free of cravings is achieved.) [29]

By practising *Vipassanā,* Siddhāttha became pure from all defilements. Since no defilements were left in him, there was no possibility of taking rebirth. Since, there was to be no rebirth, there was also no possibility of suffering from diseases, old age, death and decay, as well as parting from the pleasant ones and uniting with the unpleasant. This is known as Enlightenment. The exact state of Enlightenment cannot be described because it is beyond the cognition of senses and sensory organs. The Enlightenment can be only experienced and cannot be described. Neither can it be explained nor can it be told because it is beyond the perception of sensory organs.

The tree under which he sat came to be known as the *Bodhi-tree*, and the area near where the tree stood is known as *Bodh-gayā*.

Before the Enlightenment, Siddhāttha was only a *Bodhisatta.* It is after reaching Enlightenment that he became the Buddha. A *Bodhisatta* is a person who is seeking to be a Buddha. To become the Buddha, a *Bodhisatta* must acquire all of the following qualities such as the *Muditā* (joy), *Vimala* (purity), *Prabhākarī* (Brightness), *Arcishmati* (intelligence of fire), *Sudurjaya* (difficult to conquer), *Abhimukhī* (developing the most profound compassion in the heart), *Duraṅgama* (going far off) *Acala* (immovable), *Sādhumati* (the stage or condition of the one who has vanquished and penetrated all *Dharma-s* or systems), and *Dharmamegha* (attaining the all-penetrating eye of a Buddha). In addition to above, a *Bodhisatta* also acquires ten *Parami-s* (perfections), which are as the following : *Dāna* (generosity), *Sīla* (morality), *Nekkhamma* (renunciation), *Paññā* (wisdom), *Viriya* (energy), *Khānti* (patience), *Sacca* (truthfulness), *Adhiṭṭhāna* (determination), *Metta* (loving-kindness) and *Upekkhā* (equanimity).

It is only when one is doubly equipped that a *Bodhisatta* becomes qualified for becoming a Buddha. The Buddha is the culminating point in the life of a *Bodhisatta.* The Buddha is the highest degree of purity as the essence of being. The condition precedent for becoming a Buddha has no parallel anywhere. None of the any other teachings in the world calls upon its founder to answer such a test.

After attaining Enlightenment, Gotama the Buddha enjoyed the bliss and ecstasy for seven weeks. At the end of the seventh week, Tapussa and Bhallika, two merchants from Ukkala (an ancient city near the present day Rangoon in Myanmar) offered him rice, cakes and honey. These two became the first lay disciples (Upāsaka) of Buddha by taking refuge in *Du-ratana* (two gems) of the Buddha and the *Dhamma.* The *Saṅgha* was not yet formed. These two remained the only lay disciple who had taken *Du-ratana Sharanam.*

Buddha's Ministry

With infinite compassion and love towards all beings, the Buddha decided to preach the *Dhamma* for the welfare and happiness of all. On enquiry from wandering ascetic Upaka, he came to know that his two teachers Ālāra Kālāma and Uddaka

Ramputta had passed away. Out of gratitude, he thought of those five *Parivrājaka-s*, who served him for six months but left him when he abandoned asceticism. Upaka told him that they were meditating at the deer park (Mrigadāya vana) at Isipatana near Sarnath. He proceeded to Isipatana. When the five ascetics saw him coming, they decided not to stand and greet him as he had already abandoned the asceticism. But when the Buddha entered the gate of the deer park they were so overwhelmed by his measured steps and calm and serene appearance that they all stood up in reverence and awe at once. His eyes and smile showed the evidence of his Enlightenment. His penetrating gaze wiped out their intention of snubbing him for abandoning asceticism. Koṇḍañña ran up to him and took his alms bowl. Mahānāma fetched water so that the Buddha could wash his hands and feet, Bhaddiya prepared a seat for him, Vappa brought a fan of leaves for him, while Assaji offered him a bowl of cool water. The Buddha told them that he had discovered the Path of Liberation and he would teach them the same. After a short conversation, the five ascetics were convinced that Siddhāttha Gotama had indeed become a Buddha and they requested him to teach them the *Dhamma*.

Addressing them, the Buddha said:

"There are these two extremes (*Anta*), O *Bhikkhu-s*, which should be avoided by one who has renounced (*Pabbajitena*); and these two extremes are the following:

(i) Indulgence in sensual pleasures – this is base, vulgar, worldly, ignoble and non beneficial;

(ii) Addiction to self-mortification – this is painful, ignoble and non-beneficial.

> "Abandoning both these extremes, the *Tathāgata* has comprehended the Middle Path (*Majjhimā Paṭipadā*) which promotes sight *(Cakkhu*) and knowledge (*Ñāna*) and which tends to peace (*Upasamā*), higher wisdom (*Abhiññāya*), enlightenment (*Sambodhi*) and complete liberation (*Nibbāna)*.
>
> "The Noble Eightfold Path namely, the Path comprising the right understanding (*Sammā Diṭṭhi*), right thoughts (*Samma Sankappa*), right speech (*Sammā Vācā*), right

action (*Sammā Kammanta),* right livelihood (*Sammā Ājīva*), right effort (*Sammā Vāyāma*), right mindfulness (*Samma Sati*) and right concentration (*Sammā Samādhi*), O *Bhikkhus*, is the Middle Path which the *Tathāgata* has comprehended."

The Buddha continued:

"Now, this, O *Bhikkhu-s,* is the Noble Truth of Suffering (*Dukkha-Ariya-Sacca*)! Birth is suffering, decay is suffering; disease is suffering, death is suffering, to be united with the unpleasant is suffering, to be separated from the pleasant is suffering, not to get what one desires is suffering. In brief, the five aggregates of attachment are suffering.

Dhammacakkapavattana at Sarnath

"Now, this O *Bhikkhus,* is the Noble Truth of the Cause of Suffering (*Dukkha-Samudaya-Ariya-Sacca*):

"It is this craving which produces rebirth (*Ponobbhavika*), accompanied by passionate clinging welcoming this and that (life). It is the craving for sensual pleasures (*Kāmataṇhā*), craving for existence *(Bhavataṇhā*) and craving for non-existence (*Vibhavataṇhā*).

"Now, this O *Bhikkhu-s*, is the Noble Truth of the Cessation of Suffering *(Dukkha–Nirodha–Ariya–Sacca*):

"It is the complete separation from and destruction of this very craving, its forsaking, renunciation, the liberation there from, and non-attachment thereto.

"Now, this *O Bhikkhus* is the Noble Truth of the Path leading to the Cessation of Suffering (*Dukkha–Nirodha*

–Gāminī–Paṭipadā–Ariya–Sacca).

"It is this Noble Eightfold Path–namely, Right Understanding, Right Thoughts, Right Speech, Right Action, Right Livelihood, Right Effort, Right Mindfulness and Right Concentration.

"Thus, O *Bhikkhu-s,* with respect to things unheard before, there arose in me the eye, the knowledge, the wisdom, the insight and the light."

Concluding his discourse the Buddha said:

"As long, O *Bhikkhu-s* as the absolute true intuitive knowledge regarding these Four Noble Truths under their three aspects and twelve modes was not perfectly clear to me, so long I did not acknowledge in this world inclusive of gods, *Māra-s* and *Brahma-s* and amongst the hosts of ascetics and priests, gods and men, that I had gained the incomparable supreme Enlightenment (*Anuttaraṁ Sammā-Sambodhiṁ*).

"When, O *Bhikkhu-s,* the absolute true intuitive knowledge regarding these Four Noble Truths under their three aspects and twelve modes, became perfectly clear to me, then only did I acknowledge in this world inclusive of gods, Māra-s, Brahma-s, amongst the hosts of ascetics and priests, gods and men, that I had gained the Incomparable Supreme Enlightenment.

"And there arose in me the knowledge and insight (*Ñānadassana*).

"Unshakable is the deliverance of my mind. This is my last birth, and now there is no existence again."

The Middle Path of the Buddha

When this doctrine was being expounded there arose in the venerable Koṇḍañña the dustless, stainless, truth-seeing eye (*Dhammacakkhu*) and he saw that "whatever is subject to origination all that is subject to cessation."

Seeing the expression of venerable Koṇḍañña, the Buddha said: "Friends, Koṇḍañña knows! Koṇḍañña knows!"

Therefore, the venerable Koṇḍañña was named *Aññāta* (wise) *Koṇḍañña*. The sermon came to be known as the *Dhammacakka-pavattana-sutta* and the teaching as *Dhammacakka-pavattana* (setting the wheel of *Dhamma* in motion). It was on the full moon day of *Asadha* (June-July). According to the Pāli texts, the vibrations of *Dhammacakka- pavattana-sutta* were so powerful that the ten thousand world systems quaked, tottered and trembled with joy and ecstasy.

The five *Parivrājaka-s* felt that in him they had found a reformer, full of the most earnest moral purpose and trained in all the intellectual culture of his time, who had the originality and the courage to put forth deliberately and with a knowledge of opposing views, the doctrine of salvation to be found here, in this life, in the inward change of heart to be brought about by the practice of self-culture and self-control.

Their reverence for the Buddha became so unbounded that they at once surrendered to him and requested him to accept them as his disciples. The Buddha admitted them into his order by uttering '*Ehi Bhikkhave'* (come in Bhikkhus). They became his first five disciples and known as the *Pañcavaggiya Bhikkhus*. The Buddha told these five monks that if they practiced the *Dhamma* with an open mind and with diligence, then they could attain complete liberation from cravings, aversion and attachment in three months. The Buddha stayed in the deer park to guide these monks in practicing meditation.

The *Anatta-lakkhaṇa-sutta*, in which the Buddha preached about the impermanence and non- self nature of all things, later followed this sermon. By practicing *Vipassanā* meditation, Koṇḍañña realised the truth of the impermanence, substancelessness, and the unsatisfactory nature of reality (*Anicca, Anatta* and *Dukkha*) at the experiential level and became fully awakened. Two months later, Vappa and Bhaddiya also became liberated. Shortly after that Mahānāma and Assaji also became liberated. Thus, within three months, all the five attained *Arhantaship*. With these five *Arahantas*, the Buddha formed the *Bhikkhu Saṅgha*, a community of those who live in harmony and awareness. The *Bhikkhu Saṅgha* was a loosely knit organisation without a central authority.

Not long after this, Yasa, the depressed and mentally disturbed son of a wealthy merchant of Vārānasi, who could not find peace in his riches and way of life, approached the Buddha and received ordination. He was followed by fifty-four of his friends, who also became monks. Having tasted *Dhamma*, they soon gained the peace that they were seeking for long and with continued practice they all attained the stage of *Arahanta* (full liberation). His father and mother became the first lay disciples who took refuge in the 'triple gem,' as by then there were triple gems in which to take refuge: the *Buddha*, the *Dhamma*, and the *Saṅgha*.

The Buddha spent a rain retreat (*Varṣāvāsa)* at Saranath with the *Saṅgha* that by that time had grown to sixty *Arahanta Bhikkhu-s* (liberated monks). As the rainy season ended he instructed them as follows:

> Wander forth, O monks, for the benefit of the many, for the happiness of the many, for showering forth compassion on the world; for the good, the benefit and happiness of gods and men. Let no two go in the same direction. Teach the *Dhamma*, *Bhikkhu-s*, and meditate on the holy life. There are beings with only a little desire left within them who are languishing for lack of hearing the *Dhamma*; they will understand it.[30]

The Buddha, after having sent these sixty *Bhikkhu-s* out to various places for spreading the *Dhamma*, continued to teach these same truths himself. Thus, they all carried the torch of light, which dispels the darkness of ignorance. Their teaching did not consist of mere discourses, mere words. They explained the real meaning and essence of the words they taught. Their success in teaching the *Dhamma* lay in enabling the people to practice what was taught.

The greatest conviction and insight can be imparted by words only if the teachers are themselves practicing what they are preaching. Because they realised that the truth of the path to liberation they became shining examples of what they taught. The nature of the *Dhamma* expressed in this way is beneficial in the beginning, beneficial in the middle, and beneficial in the end. The immediate results of the theory and practice of *Dhamma* (*Pariyatti, Paṭipatti)* started to manifest. People from different sects, castes, and classes were attracted to the *Dhamma* that is universal and non-sectarian, and which gives beneficial results here and now. That is why many people, including leaders of different sects, started practising the *Dhamma.* For instance, Yasa, the three Kassapa brothers with their thousand followers became monks. Also, two Brahmins, Sāriputta and Moggallāna, took ordination, and later became the chief disciples of the Buddha.

Many other important people of that time also became attracted to the *Dhamma*: kings Bimbisāra, Suddhodana, and Prasendi; the wealthy merchants *Anāthapiṇḍika*, Jotiya, *Jaṭila*, Meṇḍaka, Puṇṇāka and Kakavaliya; and important women such as Visākhā, Suppavāsā, and Khemā. They donated various monasteries to the *Saṅgha* with the good intention that the *Dhamma* might spread throughout society. These facilities enabled people to learn and practise the *Dhamma,* and thereby come out of their suffering.

Daily Routine of the Buddha

The manner in which the Buddha spent each day was very simple. He would rise early, wash and dress himself without assistance. He would then meditate in solitude till it was time to go out for alms. When the time arrived, he would, dressed suitably, with his bowl in hand, alone or attended by some disciples, visit the neighbouring town or village. After finishing his meal from some house, he would preach the *Dhamma* to the host and his family with due regard to their capacity for spiritual enlightenment, and when done return to his lodgings and wait in the open veranda till all his followers had finished their meal. He would then retire to his private apartment and, after suggesting subjects for thought to some of his disciples, take a short rest during the heat of the day. In the afternoon he would meet the folk from neighbouring villages or town assembled in the lecture-hall, and preach them the *Dhamma* in a manner suited to their capacities. Then at the close of the day, after refreshing himself with a bath when necessary, he would explain difficulties or expound the doctrine to some of his disciples thus spending the first watch of the night. Part of the remaining night he would spend in meditation walking up and down outside his chamber, and the other part resting in his bedchamber. During the nine months of fair weather, the Buddha went from place to place walking fifteen to twenty miles a day. During the rainy season he stayed at one place normally for three months, which was known as *Vassāvāsa* (the rains retreat).

The rainy season is not a good time for travel. Therefore, the Buddha asked the *Bhikkhu-s* to stay together at one place to avoid illness from exposing themselves to the rains and also to avoid stepping on worms and other small creatures, which come up onto the ground.

The *Bhikkhu-s* could choose one of the monasteries or centres. Each centre had fixed boundaries. No *Bhikkhu* was allowed to leave the centre for more than one week during the three months of monsoon season unless there was a compelling reason. This enabled them to evolve a community life. They held simple ceremonies in the *Dhamma* Hall of the monastery/meditation centre, and the Buddha or a senior monk would instruct them about *Dhamma* every morning. If the number of monks was very large, then they were divided into sub-groups headed by a senior monk. After sermons and meditation, the monks would go out for alms in different directions. After the alms round, they would return to the *Dhamma* Hall for lunch, sharing with each other. If any monk did not get alms, then other monks would divide their alms amongst them so that he got an equal share. After eating their meal, they would take a short rest. Then they would meditate in the afternoon followed by *Dhamma* discourse by the Buddha or a senior monk.

The Buddha would also remain at one place during the rains and move around Northern India teaching *Dhamma* during the rest of the year. The period of rain retreat varied from three to five months. If the monks were able to complete *Vipassanā* meditation in three months, the rain retreat would conclude on the full moon day of the month of *Āshwin* (October), then the Buddha and his order of monks would move from one village to another, from town to town teaching *Dhamma* to common folk and lay followers for nine months. If the meditation was not completed in three months, the rain retreat would be extended for four months and after the completion ceremony on the full moon day of the month of *Kārtika* (November), the Buddha along with his *Bhikkhu Saṅgha* would start travelling on the first day of the month of *Mārgashīrsha* (December). In some cases, when meditation was not completed even in four months, the rains retreat was extended up to five months, to be concluded on the full moon day of the month of *Mārgashīrsha* (December) and travel for the remaining seven months, teaching the *Dhamma* throughout Northern India. However, the rain retreat was not extended beyond five months.

The Buddha spent the first *Vassāvāsa* (rain retreat) at Isipatana, Deer Park, Sarnath, near Vārānasi in 528 BC. He spent his second retreat in 527 BC, the third in 526 BC and the fourth in 525 BC at Rājagraha in the Bamboo grove donated by the king Bimbisāra. During this *Vassāvāsa*, Mahākāshyapa, who was the son of a very wealthy businessman of Magadha, was ordained. It was during this *Vassāvāsa* that the Buddha preached the *Rāhulovāda sutta* in which he explained the good and bad actions of mind, speech and body by comparing them with the examples of a royal elephant and a mirror. After a few days of *Vassāvāsa*, Anāthpiṇḍika, a very wealthy merchant of Sāvatthi, came to meet the Buddha, and he invited him to visit Sāvatthi.

The Buddha, after assigning the work of supervision of the newly-ordained monks to Koṇḍañña and Uruvela Kāshyapa reached Vaishāli after four months, along with five hundred monks and stayed at the Kutagira monastery at Mahāvana. The Buddha preached *Tittira Jātaka* to explain the importance of mutual respect and harmonious relationship in the community of monks. Leaving two hundred monks at the Kutagira monastery, the Buddha along with three hundred monks proceeded to Sāvatthi: Anāthpiṇḍka donated the Jetvana monastery to the *Bhikkhu Saṅgha* at Sāvatthi. The fifth rain retreat was spent in Vesālī in 524 BC. On the invitation of king Suddhodana to teach *Dhamma* to the people of Kapilavatthu, the Buddha visited Kapilavatthu.

Last Meeting with Suddhodana

News that the Buddha was residing at Rājagraha and was preaching *Dhamma* reached the ears of the aged king Suddhodana, and his anxiety to see his Enlightened son grew stronger by the day. On nine successive occasions, he sent nine courtiers, each with a large following, to invite the Buddha to Kapilavatthu. Contrary to his expectations, they all heard the *Dhamma* and attaining *Arahantahood*, entered the order. Since the *Arahanta*-s were indifferent to worldly things, they did not convey the message to the Buddha.

The disappointed king finally dispatched another faithful courtier Kāludāyī who was a playmate of prince Siddhāttha. He agreed to go as he was granted permission to enter the order.

Like the previous courtiers, he also had the fortune to attain *Arahantahood* and join the order. But unlike the others, he conveyed the message to the Buddha, and persuaded him to visit his aged father. As the season was most suitable for travelling, the Buddha, attended by the large retinue of his disciples, travelled to Kapilavatthu, preaching *Dhamma* along the way. On reaching Kapilavatthu he taught *Dhamma* to the king Suddhodana, Mahāprajāpati Gotami, Yashodharā and other members of the royal family. After hearing the discourse, they departed without extending invitation for lunch. As there was no special invitation for lunch, the Buddha and his disciples went out for alms from the houses of the citizens of Kapilavatthu.

On hearing this news, the king reached the scene and after saluting the Buddha said: "Son, why do you ruin me? I am overwhelmed with shame to see you begging alms. Is it proper for you to seek alms in this very city instead of dining with us? Why do you put me to shame?"

To this the Buddha said: "I am not putting you to shame, O great king! I am following the custom of the Buddha lineage. Several thousand Buddhas have lived by seeking alms."

The Buddha, then advised the king to be not heedless in standing (at doors for alms), he advised him to lead a righteous life to live happily. During this visit, the Buddha preached the *Dhamma* to Yashodhra, Rahul and other family members.

During this visit, thousands of *Śākyans* joined the *Saṅgha,* including his son Rāhula, and stepbrother Nanda. Others such as Anuruddha, Bhaddiya, Ānanda, Bhagu, Kimbila, Devadatta and even the royal barber Upāli joined the *Saṅgha* as well.

When the Buddha's father king Suddhodana had died, his widow Mahāpajāpati Gotami requested the Buddha to allow women to join the *Saṅgha.* Ānanda interceded on their behalf and their request was granted. This was the beginning of an order of nuns (*Bhikkhuni Saṅgha*). The Buddha delivered the *Prajāpati-sutta* or the governing behaviour and conduct of nuns.

The Buddha Banned display of Psychic Powers and Miracles

One of the Buddha's disciples, Monk Pindola Bharadwaja, displayed his psychic powers by performing a miracle. He flew in the air to bring down a sandalwood bowl hanging at the top of a bamboo stick. When the Buddha came to know about it he banned any display of psychic powers and the performance of any miracle by a Buddhist monk as it would digress from the path of liberation and make people blind followers of such miracle performers as well as superstitious. 'Those who hunger for psychic/ miraculous powers hunger for worldly gain over spiritual progress, thus failing to understand the true nature of these powers.'[30a] On hearing the news of the ban, the opponents of the Buddha plotted a conspiracy to challenge the Buddha at Sāvatthi to perform a miracle. The Buddha, seeing the necessity, accepted the challenge and performed a great miracle at Sāvatthi. Legend tells us that when the opponents challenged him, he announced that he would perform a miracle under a mango tree at a place in Sāvatthi on *Āshādi Pūrṇimā.* The opponents destroyed the mango trees from the place. On the appointed day the Buddha reached the place. The royal gardener offered him a mango fruit. The Buddha ate the fruit. He pushed the kernel in the soil and washed his hands on it. A big mango tree sprang up immediately. Two streams of water and fire sprang up from the Buddha's body along with five colours. On being asked by the king Pasenadi of Kosala, the Buddha explained to the king that this miracle was performed under very exceptional circumstances to protect the *Dhamma*.

The Buddha spent the sixth rain retreat in 523 BC at Ma*n*kulapabbata. He spent the seventh rain retreat in 522 BC at Tāvatiṁsa. Preaching Abhidhamma (higher teachings) to Mahāmāyā and other devas and from there descended to Sankissa mountains upstream from the Ganges. He spent the eighth season in 521 BC at Suṁsumāragira in Bhagga. From there he wandered onto Sāvatthi and preached to king Pasenadi of Kosala that a monk should not be judged by his age, rather by his virtues and righteous life. Even a young monk can be the master of the *Dhamma*, if he practices it correctly, he told the king. Wandering through Kosala, the Buddha proceeded to Rājagraha through Vaishāli. In that year the Buddha preached Jatila Sutta in which he explained to the monks that the *Dhamma* should be visible in their daily lives and they should be the living examples of the *Dhamma,* and told them that yellow robes alone do not make a person a monk.

The Buddha spent the ninth rain retreat in 520 BC at the

Ghosita monastery near Kosambi, which was in the midst of Siṁsapa trees. One day he took a few simsapa leaves in his hands and asked the *Bhikkhus* whether the number of leaves in his hands was greater than those in the forest. When the *Bhikkhus* replied that the number of leaves in the forest were more than those in his hands, the Buddha said, "Just so, what I see is much greater than what I teach. Why? Because I teach only those things that are truly necessary and helpful in attaining the Liberation."

That year the monks quarrelled on some issue. The dispute first started amongst the senior monks called *Sīlācāryās* (those well versed in rules of morality) and *Sūtrācāryās* (expert of discourses) and subsequently the younger monks also got divided and infighting started. When the news reached the Buddha, he advised that enmity begets enmity and it can be ended only with love and not with enmity. Negative thoughts like, 'I have been insulted', 'I have been harmed', or 'I have been humiliated', only pollute the minds and defile the purity of the mind. Those who do not pollute their mind with negative thoughts will always remain happy and blissful.

To allow monks time to sort out their differences, the Buddha left the monastery and went to Balkalonkar village to preach the *Dhamma* to Bhrigu. From there he went to Prachinvanshdav and preached to the monks Aniruddha, Nandiya, Kimbila and many others about mutual love and respect and brotherhood amongst the community of monks. He gave discourse for removing the five fetters that create impediments in the meditation process. The Buddha stayed there for one month. From there he went to the Pālileyyaka forests where he befriended wild animals by practicing meditation of loving-kindness. Elephants would bring him water and sometimes even brought flowers and fruits for him. The Buddha learned the language of the elephants and used to talk to them in their language!

The Buddha spent the tenth rain retreat in 519 BC at the Pālileyyaka forests with elephants and other wild animals. After the retreat, he went to Sāvatthi. He gave discourse at the Jetavana monastery for two weeks. By this time, the dispute among the quarrelling monks was over and they reached Sāvatthi to ask for his forgiveness. Both the *Sīlācaryas* and the *Sūtrācaryās* requested each other for forgiveness and their differences were sorted out. To solve such types of problems in future, the Buddha formulated a seven-point *Saptādhikaraṇa Samatha.* The Buddha stayed in the Jetavana monastery for six months and returned to Rājagraha via Uruvela. From there he went to Nālandā and spent his eleventh rain retreat in 518 BC at Ekanala village. By this time, twenty-four conduct rules were formulated for the monks. In the same year, the *Prātimokkha* rules were formulated, according to which, if a monk violated any of the rules of celibacy, non-stealing, non-violence and an exaggeration of his psychic achievements, then the *Bhikkhu Saṅgha* would call for a convention to discuss that violation. If any violation was found then he would be ex-communicated from the *Saṅgha.* Observation of these four major codes of conduct of monks were called the four *Pārājikas.* On every full moon day, and the new moon day, the *Bhikkhu Saṅgha* would collectively recite the conduct rule. After reciting every conduct rule, the monks would be asked whether they violated any of the rules and if everybody kept silence then the next rule would be recited. If there was any violation by any monk, he had to accept it in front of the entire *Saṅgha,* after which the monk was forgiven.

During that year, the Buddha preached *Asibandhaka-putta-sutta* at Nālandā, in which he explained the eight causes which destroy a family. In the same year, he preached *Nigantha Sutta* in which he explained the consequences of not following the path of morality and right conduct. From there, he went to Pañcashāla village in Magadha and preached *Piṇda Sutta*. From there, the Buddha embarked on to Kammasadamma in the Kuru country (modern Haryana) and preached the *Mahāsatipaṭṭhānasutta*. There a Brahmin named Māgandiya offered his most beautiful and homely daughter to the Buddha. The Buddha politely told him that he has fully liberated himself from sensual pleasures. The Buddha explained the four *Smriti-Prasthāna* of *Mahāsatipaṭṭhāna* namely, *Kāyānupassanā, Vedanānupassanā, Cittānupassanā and Dhammānupassanā,* which helps in liberating one from attachment towards sensual pleasures. After some time the Buddha gave discourse on *Mahānidāna-sutta a*t the same place, in which the Law of Dependent Arising was explained in detail. From

Kammāsadamma, the Buddha proceeded to Verañja via Mathurā. On his way, he gave discourse on the relationship of husband and wife especially about how to improve it.

The Buddha spent the twelfth rain retreat in 517 BC at Verañja, giving discourse on the *Verañjaka-sutta* in which he explained *Kriyāvāda* (action), *Akriyāvāda* (non-action) and *Ucchedavāda* (extinction). One day, Arahata-Sāriputta suggested that the conduct rules followed by the monks needed to be refined and reduced to writing. The Buddha replied that the time had not yet come. Twelve years ago when the order of monks was formed there were only five conduct rules, which had now grown to hundred and twenty. In the coming years, these might go up to two hundred. It was more important to abide by the conduct rules than remembering them and advising others by writing them down, the Buddha told *Arahata* Sāriputta. After the rain retreat, the Buddha travelled towards the south, reaching Sankisa (near modern day Kannauj) in Uttar Pradesh. Roaming through central Uttar Pradesh, he crossed the Ganges and reached Vaishāli via Vārānasi. There he stayed at the Kuṭāgara monastery at Mahāvana.

The Buddha spent the thirteenth rain retreat in 516 BC at the Cālika mountains. Up till now, the monk Meghiya had accompanied the Buddha as his personal assistant. But Meghiya's mind used to waver during the meditations. He wanted to meditate in solitude. The Buddha explained that meditation in solitude does not imply keeping oneself away from the help of friends. The monks were kept in the order for this very purpose: they could help each other. The Buddha taught him the importance of affection, harmony, mutual love, being scrupulous in studying the *Dhamma Sutta,* practicing meditation with diligence and direct experiential wisdom.

After the retreat the Buddha went to Vaishāli and stayed at the Kuṭāgara monastery. There he gave discourse on the *Saptangika Sutta* to the commander of Licchavies about how to defend his republic. In the same year, he ordained Meṇḍaka, a house holder. From there the Buddha went to a forest in the north of the Mahi river, where he gave discourse on the *Potaliya Sutta,* explaining the importance of the eight moral precepts for a happy life.

While roaming in the Aṅguatarraye area, the Buddha preached

the *Saila Sutta* to a Brahmin named Sail and his three hundred disciples. From there he wandered to Kushinārā, accompanied by twelve hundred and fifty monks. The Mallas of Kushinārā welcomed the Buddha with a lot of enthusiasm. From Kushinārā, the Buddha wandered to Ātuma town and stayed at the Bhusāgāra monastery. From there he wandered to Sāvatthi and stayed at the Jetavan monastery. There he preached the *Cula-Hastipadopama-Sutta* to Jānushroni Brahmins in which the importance of the life of a *Bhikkhu* and the benefits of morality and right conduct were thoroughly explained. At the end of the discourse, Jānushroni Brahmin opted for ordination and entered the order of the monks. During the same year, Ashwālāyana and five hundred other Brahmins were given the discourse on the *Assalāyana-sutta,* in which the uselessness and defects of the *Varṇāshrama* system were explained.

The Buddha spent the fourteenth rain retreat in 515 BC at the Jetavana monastery in Sāvatthi. During that year, he gave discourse on the *Mahārāhulovāda-sutta* in which the impermanence and selflessness of six sensory organs and their objects, and also on the delusions about the existence of soul was explained. He explained to Rahul that the five physical senses such as *Rūpa (*body), *Vedanā* (sensation), *Saññā* (senses), *Saṁkhāra* (imprints in the mind) and *Viññāna* (consciousness) are neither permanent nor perpetual and that there is nothing like the soul. About the soul, he said there are three delusions. The first delusion is the belief that the body, its consciousness, its cognition, its sensations and *Saṁkhāra* are souls and the soul takes rebirth. The second delusion is accepting that these five physical senses are not the soul, or the soul is a different entity from these physical senses or the physical senses are under the control of the soul. As the decay of the five bodily senses happens automatically, no one can control this decay. Thinking that the soul is present in these physical senses is the third delusion. The meditation on the non-existence of soul means impermanence of the five physical senses, concentrating on the sorrows caused by them, which can be known by perception that neither there is any soul nor there is any relationship between the soul and other sensory organs and their consciousness. Neither the soul nor the five physical senses and their consciousness are under control of each other.

The next day while giving discourse on self-reliance and importance of living in the present moment, the Buddha explained about the importance of self-reliance and the best way to lead a solitary life. A self-reliant person is the one who always remains in a state of consciousness, say for instance, knowing what is happening at the present moment or what should be done to each entity. He neither goes into the past nor does he get himself embroiled in the delusions of the future because the past is gone and the future is a distant dream. Everything that is in life is the present moment because we have to live this moment. If we lose the present, we lose our life. This is the best way to live a solitary life.

During that year, the Buddha preached the *Ankkhan Sutta* at the Jetavana monastery. Not long before that he stayed at Tindukachiraram, which was constructed and donated by the queen Mallikā of Sāvatthi. The Buddha preached the *Poṭṭhapāda Sutta* in which he explained the Law of Dependent Arising and the benefit of a monk's life and also explained the delusions about the theory of the soul. From Sāvatthi, the Buddha wandered to Mansakat village on the bank of the Acairvati river and preached the *Tevijja Sutta* to Vashishṭha and Bharadwāja in which he explained how by practicing a life of morality, mastery over mind and direct experiential wisdom, one can reach the state of Brahma.

From there the Buddha wandered to Icchangala village and stayed in the forest nearby. There he preached the *Ambattha Sutta* to Ambashta Brahmin in which he explained the baseless nature of the Varnāshrama system which preaches the superiority of one class over another class. The Buddha explained the importance of a casteless society and the bliss of a liberated life. As a consequence of this discourse, a large number of Brahmins became the lay followers of the Buddha. From there, the Buddha wandered to Opsad village in the Kosala country and preached the *Canki Sutta* in which he questioned the immortality of the *Vedas* and likened it to a blind man leading another blind man. After this discourse, a large number of Brahmins of the Kosala area became his lay followers.

From the kosala country he went to Magadha and stayed at

the mango grove of Khānumata village. There he preached the *Kutadanta Sutta* in which he explained the importance of building a healthy economy to improve the overall law and order. From there, he wandered to Champa at the bank of the Ghagra river and preached the *Sonadanda Sutta* in which he explained that one becomes a Brahmin by his good actions and not by the caste in which he was born into and he is bound to till death. From there he wandered to Vaishāli and stayed at the Kutagira monastery. There he preached the *Mahāli Sutta* explaining the direct experience of mastery over mind, divine appearance, the stages of stream earner, once returner, non-returner and *Arahata* and the stages of mind and matter. During this period, he also preached the *Tevijja Vaccha Gotta Sutta* in which he explained the characteristics of *Arahata*, his achievements, his psychic powers and the importance of morality and right conduct in the household life.

From Vaishāli, the Buddha reached Kapilavatthu and spent the fifteenth rain retreat at Nyagrodharama in Kapilavatthu in 514 BC. In the same year the sermon of the *Bharandu Sutta* and the *Mahānāma Sutta* was preached to Mahānāma, in which the Buddha explained the defilements of the mind, its bad effects and the way to purify the mind. In that very year a dispute regarding distribution of the waters from the Rohini river again erupted which turned into a fight and the Buddha had to mediate between concerned parties and the matter was solved through consultation. In Kapilavatthu he made the rule for the *Bhikkhus* against accepting more than three *Civaras* (robes).

Roaming through Kitagiri (Kerakat in Jaunpur district of the present day Uttar Pradesh) the Buddha reached Ālavi (the present day Arval in Kanpur district). He spent his sixteenth rain retreat in 513 BC at Ālavi. There he preached the *Kitagiri Sutta* and resided at *Aggala Caitya*. In the same year, the venerable Ānanda gave the discourse on the *Sandaka Sutta* to Sandak and his friends regarding four false perceptions after which they all entered the order of monks.

During that year, the Buddha preached the *Sigālo Sutta* to a young householder Sigala in which he explained the responsibilities of a householder towards parents, spouse, children, friends and relatives, neighbours, teachers, employer and employee and how to live a happy family life. After visiting Ālavi, the Buddha reached Rājagraha and moved onto Veluvana.

The Buddha spent the seventeenth rain retreat in 512 BC at Rājagraha. There he preached the *Culakāludayi-sutta,* which explains the principles of *Parivrājaka* and that of *Nigantha Putta.* From there he reached Gargarapushkarini (the Ghagra river) of Campā and traveled around there. There he preached the *Diṭṭhiva-sutta* about laws of the nature and importance of right conduct for a happy life. From there, the Buddha wandered to Ashvapura town in the *Aṅga* country and preached the *Cula-Assapura-sutta* in which he explained the meaning of *Samaṇa* and Brahmin. From there, he wandered to Kajaṅgala (district Santhal Pargana) and preached the *Indriya-Bhāvanā- sutta* in which he explained the difference between the control of senses by an *Arahata* and by a householder and how to liberate oneself from the defilements of the mind by doing *Vipassanā*. From there the Buddha wandered to the Suhya country (part of Hazaribagh and Santhal Pargana districts) and after staying there for some time, he left for the Cāliya mountains through Setkanik of Sīlavatī.

The Buddha spent the eighteenth rain retreat in 511 BC and the nineteenth one in 510 BC on the Cāliya mountains, while the twentieth rain retreat was spent in 509 BC at Vulture's Peak at Rājagraha. That year, the royal physician Jeewak attended the *Bhikkhu Saṅgha* and suggested how to improve medical facilities and medical care of the *Bhikkhu Saṅgha.*

The Buddha spent the twenty-first rain retreat in 508 BC at the Jetavana monastery at Sāvatthi, when two very important decisions were taken by the *Bhikkhu Saṅgha.* First, it was decided that henceforth the Buddha would spend every rain retreat at Sāvatthi and secondly, the venerable Ānanda would serve as personal assistant to the Buddha. Ānanda was known for his razor sharp mind, superb memory and meticulousness. Therefore, it was thought that he would remember the preaching of the Buddha verbatim. Accordingly, the Buddha spent the twenty-first to the forty-sixth rain retreats (from 508 to 484 BC) at Sāvatthi at the *Jetavana Vihāra* and *Pubbārāma Vihāra*.

During those years, he preached very important *Suttas* like the *Kālāma Sutta, Kesaputtiya Sutta, Ālavaka Sutta, Raṭṭhapāla Sutta,*

Sundarī Sutta, Brāhmaṇa-Dhammiya Sutta, Aṅgulimāla Sutta, Sunak Sutta, Doṇa Sutta, Sahassabhikkhuni Sutta, Sundarika-Bharadwāja Sutta, Udāna Sutta, Attadīpa Sutta, Mallikā Sutta, Sona Sutta, Jaṭila Sutta, Piyajātika Sutta, Puṇṇā Sutta, Sāriputta Sutta, Makhādeva Sutta, Thapati Sutta, Visākha Sutta, Padhāniya Sutta, Jarā Sutta, Bodhi-Rājakumāra Sutta, Kannatthalaka-sutta, Devadutta Sutta, Saṅgāgama Sutta, Kosala Sutta, Baheetik Sutta, Chaṅkamā Sutta, Upāli Sutta, Abhayarajakumāra Sutta, Samaṇa Sutta, Dhamma-Cetiya Sutta, Saamgaam Sutta, Saṅgīti-Pariyāya Sutta, Cunda Sutta, Ukkācela Sutta and thousands of other *Suttas*.

The Buddha taught the *Dhamma* with infinite compassion towards all beings for forty-five years. He relentlessly spread the message of liberty, equality and fraternity amongst people, harmony with nature, equitable distribution of national wealth, empowerment of women, importance of virtuous life, rational thinking and how to live a healthy, happy and peaceful life. He brought a silent and non violent revolution in the society, which was unheard of before.

Throughout his life he continually faced opposition from those espousing old superstitions and false values based on birth, caste, class, animal sacrifice etc. At times he faced great opposition from sectarian elements who tried to discredit him and his teachings by trying to create scandals. Devadatta, for instance, tried to create a schism in the *Saṅgha* and even tried to kill the Buddha by various means. In all instances, the Buddha used his infinite wisdom, love and compassion to overcome those opposing forces, and continued to serve the suffering humanity.

The Mahāparinibbāna

In 483 BC, when the Buddha was nearing the age of eighty, he visited Vesālī where the courtesan Ambapāli offered him a meal and gifted the Ambalaṭṭhika grove to the *Saṅgha*. Through the practice of *Dhamma* she came out of immorality, established herself in truth, and became an *Arahanta*. Later in the same year, he visited Pāvā and stayed in the mango grove of Cunda. Here he took a special dish called *sukaramaddava* prepared of mushrooms picked from a sandalwood tree and became ill. But even with his weak health he continued on to Kusinārā.

On his recovery, Ānanda asked the Buddha about his instructions for the Bhikkhu Saṅgha after his Mahāparinibbāna. The Buddha replied that his role had been to show the path of Dhamma. After his Mahāparinibbāna his followers were to do the same as during his life time– they were each to seek no external refuge and were to work out their own salvation by walking the path of Dhamma. He exhorted the monks:

> *'Attadipa! viharatha, attasaraṇā anaññasaraṇā; dhammadipā viharatha, dhammasaraṇā, anaññasaraṇā*[31]
>
> (Therefore, Ānanda, be your own island. Take refuge in yourselves. Seek no external refuge. Live with the Dhamma as your island, the Dhamma as your refuge. Take no external refuge. Be island unto yourselves).

On reaching Kusinārā, the Buddha instructed Ānanda to spread his upper robe between twin Sāla trees, and informed him that he would achieve *Mahāparinibbāna* by passing away. A large number of monks and lay followers assembled around him to pay their last respects. The Buddha gave them his last preaching, or *Pacchimā-Vācā*, as it is called:

Mahāparinibbāna of the Buddha

Vayadhammā Saṅkhāra, Appamādena Sampādetha.[32]

(Decay is inherent in all component things, work out your own salvation with diligence.)

Having given his last advice to his followers, the Buddha went beyond any state known to human beings. Some monks who had not achieved the *Arahata* state yet, wept in sorrow. While the gods rejoiced, the earth system shook, the *mandārava* blossoms and other flowers thickly carpeted the area between the two sal trees[33], the Buddha passed away experiencing the supreme state of being and the final goal of humanity:

As a flame blown out by the wind
Goes to rest and cannot be defined,
So the enlightened man freed from selfishness
Goes to rest and cannot be defined.
Gone beyond all images –
Gone beyond the power of words.[34]

In this way, teaching the *Dhamma* as he himself practiced it, giving the message of morality, truth, compassion, equality, liberty, brotherhood and universal love, the Buddha attained *Mahāparinibbāna* in his eightieth year, on the full moon day of Vesākha month in 483 BC.

As per the directions of the venerable Ānanda, the Mallas of Kushinārā wrapped the body of the Buddha in a new cloth, then in cotton wool, then again in a new cloth and cotton wool and so on and on till they wrapped the body in five hundred successive layers of both kinds. Then they placed the body in a vessel of iron with oil, which was placed in another larger iron vessel with oil. Then they built a great funeral pyre of fragrant woods to treat the remains of Tathāgata as the king of kings. They paid honour, reverence, last respects and homage to the remains of the Tathāgata with dancing, hymns, music, garlands and perfumes for six days.

On the seventh day, eight Malla chieftains, acting as pallbearers, carried the mortal remains of the Buddha to the shrine of the Mallas called *Makuṭa Bandhana,* and cremated it by setting afire the pyre. The Mallas collected the ashes and bones and placed them in their council hall and honoured them with dance, song, music, garlands and perfumes for seven days. The delegations from neighbouring kingdoms of Magadha, Vesālī, Śākya, Koliya, Bulaya, Pāvā and

Veṭha also arrived to pay their last respects. They divided the relics into eight portions so that the people of Magadha could build a *Stupa* in Rājagraha, the Licchavis in Vesālī, the Śākyans in Kapilavatthu, the Bulis in Allakappa, the Koliyas in Rāmagāma, the Vethans in Vethadipa, and the Mallas in both Kusinārā and Pāvā. Later on, Ashoka the Great constructed eighty-four thousand *Stupas* throughout India to motivate the people to walk on the path of *Dhamma*.

The Buddha taught *Dhamma* out of love and compassion for all beings in the common language, *Pāli*, in his unique style. The same are described in brief in the next chapter.

Chapter 2
Preachings of the Buddha

The Buddha preached the *Dhamma* to millions of people including King Suddhodana, Mahāpajāpati Gotami, Yasa and his friends, Kassapa Brothers, Sāriputta and Moggallāna, Yasodharā, Rāhula, Nanda, Ānanda, Devadatta, Anāthapiṇḍika, Visākhā, King Bimbisāra, King Prasenjita of Kosala, barber Upāli, sweeper Sunita, Sopāka, Suppiya, Sumaṅgala, a number of women like Caṇḍālikā, Prākruti, Āmrapāli, robber Aṅgulimālā, physician Jīvaka and countless others. His followers were from all classes and of different socio-economic status, coming from different backgrounds. But they all enjoyed equal status with him.

Preaching Technique

The Buddha's method of exposition was unique. He preached the *Dhamma* in the form of sermons. He spoke to a large audience composed of all those who desired to hear him. He spoke in a manner intelligible to all, and tried by frequent repetitions to impress his meaning on the least attentive minds and the most rebellious memories. He adapted himself to the capacities of his listeners. He first talked about the merits obtained in alms giving, about the duties of morality, about future happiness, about the danger, the vanity and the defilement of lusts, and about the blessings of the abandonment of lusts. When he saw that the mind of his listeners was prepared, unprejudiced, impressionable, free from hindrances to the comprehension of the Truth, elated and believing, then he preached the special doctrine of the Buddha, namely, Suffering, the Cause of Suffering, the Cessation of Suffering, and the Path to Liberation. He used to pick up the incidents from daily life to explain the *Dhamma*. Some of these stories are as follows:

The Story of the Elephant called Pāveyyaka

The Buddha used to teach the meditators from normal day events. One such event was the incident of King Prasenjita's elephant getting stuck into the mire of a pond:

King Pasenadi (in Sanskrit Prasenjita) of Kosala had an elephant called Pāveyyaka,[1] who was famous for extraordinary courage, power, bravery and wisdom. The elephant was the king's pride. He led the king to many victories in the battlefields. He had a record of not losing even a single battle. The enemy armies plotted a number of conspiracies to kill the elephant, but failed. It was said that once the king was atop that elephant, nobody could defeat him. Whenever the elephant trumpeted there was fear and chaos in the enemy camps. As time passed the elephant grew old. One day the elephant went to a pond near Sāvatthi to bathe and got stuck in the mire. The elephant tried and tried to come out of the mire, but the more he tried the more he found himself stuck. His trainers tried all sorts of tricks by offering him sugarcane, bananas, green grass to allure him, as priests allure us with the allurement of heaven, but they failed. Then they tried to threaten him by way of beating with bamboo sticks, iron rods and chains as priests threaten us with fear of going to hell. The more they tried to allure him and punish him, he got stuck deeper and deeper in the mire. Hearing the pain and bad condition of his dear elephant, the king came near the pond to see the evacuation operation. Since he came to the pond, a large number of people also gathered as the news spread like a wild fire. The Buddha was staying in the Anāthapiṇḍika's Jeta- Vana Vihara at Sāvatthi. The news reached the Buddha also. He deputed the old elephant trainer of Pāveyyaka who had also grown old and having retired from the service, was in the refuge of the Buddha. When the old elephant trainer reached near the pond and saw the elephant stuck in the mire, he laughed. Then he asked the new elephant trainers to play the bugle, which is played at the beginning of a battle. Hearing the bugle, the elephant trumpeted with a force that the people had not heard in years and came out of the mire with ease. When some *Bhikkhus* brought this news to the Buddha and asked him to explain the conduct of the old trainer, the Buddha told them that the trainer laughed wondering how this brave elephant could forget his high status and get stuck in a mire. He played the bugle to remind the elephant of his true nature and his true potential. On hearing the sound of a war bugle the elephant got out immidiately by concentrating his entire energy on getting out of the mire. The Buddha exhorted the monks saying '*Bhikkhus*! Learn something from the old elephant'. If the elephant could free himself from the mire, why can't you free yourself from the mire of craving and aversion. You can do it provided you concentrate and focus your entire energy to liberate yourself as did the old elephant.

The moral of the story is that the Buddhas, the real masters, remind the people of their true nature and true potential. They only guide people, but the people have to work out their own salvation. They neither offer you allurement of heaven nor threaten you with the punishment of hell. They only guide the people to walk on the right path of *Dhamma* so that the people come out of the suffering and miseries of life. It also tells us that howsoever strong one may be, old age will make him weak. It also illustrates as to how rich become poor and powerful become powerless one day. The habits, which we develop during our youth and in the prime years of our life continue during old age also. This elephant must have been visiting the pond in his young age also. But since he had a lot of power and energy he didn't get stuck in those days. As we grow old our power and energy gets depleted to fight against the habits of craving and aversion but the vices which we develop at a young age get stronger and stronger in old age. The story tells us to rely on that master who helps us in realising our true nature and true potential for working out our own liberation, and not on the masters who offer a shortcut and easy solutions in the name of rewards in future births ignoring our present problems.

To Walk on the Path

Once the Buddha was staying at Sāvatthi, in the Pubbārāma of Migāra's mother Vishākā.[2] A large number of people used to come to meditate and to lisen to his *Dhamma* Sermons. Every evening one young man named Brahmin Moggallāna, the accountant used to come to hear his discourses. For years he came to listen to the Buddha but never put any of the teachings into practice.

One day, after a few years, this man came a little early and found the Buddha alone. He approached him and said, “Sir, I have a question that keeps arising in my mind, raising doubts.”

“Oh? There should not be any doubts on the path of *Dhamma*; have them clarified. What is your question?” asked the Buddha.

“Sir, for many years now I have been coming to your meditation centre, and I have noticed that there are a large number of recluses around you, monks and nuns, and a still larger number of lay people, both men and women. For years some of them have been coming to you. Some of them, I can see, have certainly reached the final stage; quite obviously they are fully liberated. I can also see that others have experienced some change in their lives. They are better than they were before, although I cannot say that they are fully liberated. But sir, I also notice that a large number of people, including myself, are as they were, or sometimes they are even worse. They have not changed at all, or have not changed for the better.”

“Why should this be, sir? People come to you, such a great man, fully enlightened, such a powerful, compassionate person. Why don’t you use your power and compassion to liberate them all?”

“The Buddha smiled and said, “Young man, where do you live? What is your native place?”

“Sir, I live here in Sāvatthi, this capital city of the state of Kosala.”

“Yes, but your facial features show that you are not from this part of the country. Where are you from originally?” asked the Buddha.

“Sir, I am from the city of Rājagraha, the capital of the state of Magadha. I came and settled here in Sāvatthi a few years back.”

“And have you severed all connections with Rājagraha?” “No sir, I still have relatives there. I have friends there, I

have business there.”

“Then certainly you must go from Sāvatthi to Rājagraha quite often?”

“Yes sir. Many times each year I visit Rājagraha and return to Sāvatthi.”

“Having travelled and returned so many times on the path from here to Rājagraha, certainly you must know the path very well?"

"Oh yes, sir, I know it perfectly. I might almost say that even if I was blindfolded I could find the path to Rājagraha, so many times have I walked it."

"And your friends, those who know you well, certainly they must know that you are from Rājagraha and have settled here? They must know that you often visit Rājagraha and return, and that you know the path from here to Rājagraha perfectly?"

"Oh yes, sir. All those who are close to me know that I often go to Rājagraha and that I know the path perfectly."

"Then it must happen that some of them come to you and ask you to explain to them the path from here to Rājagraha. Do you hide anything or do you explain the path to them clearly?"

"What is there to hide, sir? I explain it to them as clearly as I can, you start walking towards the east and then head towards Benaras, and continue onward until you reach Gayā and then Rājagraha. I explain it very plainly to them, sir."

"And these people to whom you give such clear explanation, do all of them reach Rājagraha automatically without travelling on that path?"

"How can that be, sir? Those who walk the entire path to its end, only they will reach Rājagraha".

"This is what I want to explain to you, young man. People keep coming to me knowing that this is someone who has walked the path from here to *Nibbāna* and so knows it perfectly. They come to me and ask, 'What is the path to *Nibbāna,* to Liberation?' And what is there to hide? I explain it to them clearly: 'This is the path'. If somebody just nods his head and says, 'Well said, well said, a very good path, but I won't take a step on it; a wonderful path, but I won't take the trouble to walk on it', then how can such a person reach the final goal?"

"I do not carry anyone on my shoulders to take him to the final goal. Nobody can carry anyone else on his shoulders to the final goal. At most, with love and compassion one can say, "Well, this is the path, and this is how I have walked on it. You also work, you also walk, and you will reach the final goal.' But each person has to walk himself, has to take every step on the path himself. He who has taken one step on the path is one step nearer the goal. He who has taken a hundred steps is a hundred steps nearer the goal. He who has taken all the steps on the path has reached the final goal. You have to walk on the path yourself."

The Pebbles and the Ghee

The Buddha explained in the *Paṭhama-Mahānāma-Sutta*[3] by the simile of an earthen pot filled partly with gravel and stones and partly with fat and butter as to how our actions decide the future existence.

One day a young man came to the Buddha crying ceaselessly; he could not stop.

The Buddha asked him. "What is wrong, young man?"

"Sir, yesterday my old father died."

"Well, what can be done? If he has died, crying will not bring him back."

"Yes, sir, that I understand; crying will not bring back my father. But I have come to you, sir, with a special request: please do something for my dead father!"

"Oh ! Tell me, what can I do for your dead father?"

"Sir, please do something. You are such a powerful person, certainly you can do it. Look, these priestlings, pardoners, and alms-gatherers perform all sorts of rites and rituals to help the dead. And as soon as the ritual is performed here, the gateway of the kingdom of heaven is breached and the dead person receives entry there; he gets an entry visa. You, sir, are so powerful! If you perform a ritual for my dead father, he will not just receive an entry visa, he'll be granted a permanent stay! Please sir, do something for him!"

The poor fellow was so overwhelmed by grief that he could not follow any rational argument. The Buddha had to use another way to help him understand. So he said to him. "All right. Go to the market and buy two earthen pots." The young man was very happy, thinking that the Buddha had agreed to perform a ritual for his father. He ran to the market and returned with two pots.

"All right," the Buddha said, "fill one pot with ghee, with butter." The young man did it. "Fill the other with pebbles." He did that too. "Now close their mouths; seal them properly." He did it.

"Now place them in the pond over there." The young man did so, and both of the pots sank to the bottom. "Now," said the Buddha. "Bring a big stick; strike and break open the pots." The young man was very happy, thinking that the Buddha was performing a wonderful ritual for his father.

Taking a stick as the Buddha said, the young man struck hard and broke open both the pots. At once the butter contained in one pot came up and started floating on the surface of the water. The pebbles in the other pot remained at the bottom. Then the Buddha said, "Well, young man, this much I have done. Now call all your priest-lings and miracle workers and tell them to start chanting and praying: 'Oh pebbles, come up, come up! Oh butter, go down, go down!" Let me see how it happens."

"Oh sir, you have started joking! How is it possible, sir? The pebbles are heavier than water, they are bound to stay at the bottom. They can't come up, sir; this is the law of nature! The butter is lighter than water, it is bound to remain on the surface. It can't go down, sir; this is the law of nature!"

"Young man, you know so much about the law of nature, but you have not understood this natural law; if all his life your father performed deeds that were heavy like pebbles, he is bound to go down; who can bring him up? And if all his actions were light like this butter, he is bound to go up; who can pull him down? The earlier we understand the law of nature and start living in accordance with the law, the sooner we come out of our misery."[6]

Some of His Prominent Followers

People from all walks of life, including kings, nobles, traders, women, untouchables and ascetics became followers of the Buddha. While the number of *Bhikkhus* in his order was only in thousands, the householders were in millions. They also benefited by walking on the path of *Dhamma.* Given below are some brief stories of a few of his prominent followers :

King Bimbisāra

The ruler of the Magadha empire, with its capital at Rājagraha, was the first royal patron of the Buddha. Siddhāttha Gotama came to Rājagraha after the Great Renunciation. King Bimbisāra tried to persuade Gotama to return to family life and offered him half of his kingdom. Gotama refused the offer, but promised to return to Rājagraha after Enlightenment.

In pursuance of the promise, the Buddha went from Gayā to Rājagraha along with one thousand two hundred and fifty *Bhikkhus*, who included the Kassapa brothers, Sāriputta and Moggallāna. King Bimbisāra came along with thousands of his subjects to welcome the Buddha. Seeing the Buddha and Uruvela Kassapa together some of his subjects were confused as to who was the teacher and who was the follower. To clarify the confusion Uruvela Kassapa fell on the feet of the Buddha, acknowledging him as his teacher. He explained that he preferred the passionless and peaceful state of *Nibbāna* to worthless sensual pleasures and, therefore, accepted the Buddha as his supreme teacher. Thereafter, the Buddha preached *Dhamma* to the gathering. King Bimbisāra and many of his subjects attained *Sotapatti*. They took refuge in the triple gems and became lay followers. King Bimbisāra invited the Buddha and the *Bhikkhu Saṅgha* to his palace for the meal.

The Buddha entered the palace with his *bhikkhus*. King Bimbisāra, accompanied by six thousand attendants and guests, came out to welcome them. The king led the Buddha and the *Bhikkhus* to the royal courtyard where spacious tents had been set up to shade the guests from the hot sun. The Buddha was given the place of honour at the center of the courtyard. All the places for the *Bhikkhus* had been prepared with utmost care. Once the Buddha was seated, the king invited others to be seated. 'The king personally placed vegetarian food into the Buddha's bowl.'[4] Perfect silence was maintained throughout the meals. All six thousand guests were impressed by the calm and joyous countenance of the Buddha and the *Bhikkhu Saṅgha.* After the Buddha and the *Bhikkhus* finished their meal, their bowls were taken and washed and then returned. The Buddha preached the five precepts to the king and his guests.

After the discourse was over, the king requested the Buddha to accept a gift of *Veluvana* (bamboo forest), which was a secluded place, neither too far nor too close to the city, accessible to those who desired to visit him, pleasant, not crowded during the day, not too noisy at night, airy and fit for the privacy of *Bhikkhus,* for the use of the Buddha and the *Saṅgha*. The park with this ideally secluded bamboo grove, also known as 'The Sanctuary of the Squirrels,' was filled with many shady trees and secluded spots.

This was the first gift of a place of residence for the Buddha and His disciples. The Buddha spent three successive rainy seasons and subsequently three other rainy seasons in quiet Veluvanārāma.

Anāthapiṇḍika (Sudatta)

Sudatta was a very wealthy merchant of Kosala.[5] He was a resident of Sāvatthi. He came in contact with the Buddha when he went to visit in laws at Rājagraha. He heard the discourse of the Buddha that nothing happens without a cause and that the Law of Dependent Origination operates in the universe. He asked the Buddha whether he should renunciate wordly life to seek liberation. The Buddha told him that *Dhamma* is available to every person irrespective of whether he is a householder or a monk. Whoever follows the noble Eight fold Path can achieve Liberation. One who has money and property and uses it rightfully for the welfare of his family, friends and relatives and for the human beings remains in bliss. Whatever is one's profession whether service or trade or industry or self- employment, one should do it honestly, sincerely and with full dedication. Such a person is like a lotus flower who remains in the water but the water never touches it. Anāthapiṇḍika realized that the *Dhamma* taught by the Tathāgata was universal and eternal. He realized that the four Noble Truths and the noble Eight fold Path of *Sīlā, Samādhi* and *Paññā* are real remedies for the sufferings of the world. He requested Lord Buddha to come to Sāvatthi (Shrāvasti) where he wanted to construct a meditation centre. Seeing his dedication the Buddha accepted the offer with a smile. Anāthapiṇḍika returned to Sāvatthi and started looking for a suitable place which should neither be very far away from the city nor very close to the city so that there would be no problem of conveyance and disturbance due to noise. The only suitable site that could be found near Sāvatthi was the pleasure park of prince Jeta, son of king Pasenadi. Jeta refused to sell the place. Seeing the determination of Anāthapiṇḍika and not knowing how to avoid him, he told him that he had to spread the gold coins on the land. Anāthapiṇḍika accepted the offer.

Anāthpiṇḍika spreading the gold coins at Jeta's Park

He started bringing cartloads of gold coins and spreading them in the park. When he had spread 180 million gold coins in two-thirds of the park, prince Jeta asked him the purpose for which he was paying such a high price. When Anāthapiṇḍika told him that he wanted to construct a monastery where the Buddha would teach the *Dhamma,* the prince donated the rest of the land. Anāthapiṇḍika spent 180 million gold coins to construct a huge Vipassanā Meditation Centre. The Buddha spent many Vassāvāsa (rain retreats) at Jetavana Vihāra.

Patācārā

There was a very rich trading family in Sāvatthi. They had one son and a daughter. The parents were busy in earning money and therefore, they had no time for their growing children. The daughter got involved with the domestic servant. When she was twenty she was engaged to an eligible bachelor. On the day of her marriage she ran away with the servant. She delivered a son after two years. After some time she again conceived. By this time she had become very poor and decided to return home. On the night when she was returning, there was thunder and downpour. On the way, she went into labour. Her husband went in search of wood and leaves for construction of a temporary hut, but he was bitten

The Buddha teaching Dhamma to Patācārā

by a snake and died on the spot, leaving her to deliver her baby on her own. Crying with her sons, she proceeded to Sāvatthi. She had to cross the swelling Aciravatī river (now known as Rāpti). She could not manage to cross the river with both sons. Therefore, she decided to first cross with her younger son and then bring the elder son. She crossed the river and laid her younger son on the other bank of the river. When she was coming to take the elder son with her and reached midstream, an eagle swooped down and carried off the youngest son, and in a frenzy, she waved her arms frantically to frighten the bird. The elder son, thinking this was a signal to come, jumped into the river and was carried away by the current. The helpless mother was left only to cry inconsolably. Crying, she proceeded to Sāvatthi. On the way, she crossed the crematorium and found that all her family members had been killed as the house had collapsed due to heavy rains the previous night and they all were cremated together. Hearing this, she went mad. She tore all her clothes and became fully naked. She was running on the streets of Sāvatthi only to be attacked by the lumpen elements and kids with stones shouting "Crazy! Crazy!"

One day when the Buddha was teaching *Dhamma* at Jetvana

Vihāra, she passed by. Hearing the voice of Buddha, she also joined the gathering and came to her senses. Realising that she was totally naked, she felt ashamed and tried to cover her body with her hands. One Upasaka spread a bed sheet upon her and that is how she came to be known as *'Paṭācārā'*[6] (the lady covered with a bed sheet).

The Buddha called her near him and taught her the *Dhamma.* She realized the *Anicca* (impermanence). She was ordained and admitted to the *Bhikkhuni Saṅgha* (the order of nuns). Patācārā devoted the rest of her life to the service of suffering humanity. Walking on the path of *Dhamma* she attained *Sotāpanna* (stream enterer), which is the first stage of nibbanic bliss.

Kisā Gotami

Gotami Tissa was a girl from a very poor and downtrodden family of Sāvatthi. As she was very slim, her name became Kisā (*Krishā*). She was married into a rich family. Since her parents were poor, she was not respected in her in-laws' home. She was humiliated and insulted on the slightest pretext. For years after her marriage, Kisā Gotami suffered the painful burden of childlessness. After some time, she gave birth to a beautiful son, who brought her honour and respect from her in-laws. Overnight she became the blue-eyed girl of her in-laws. But unfortunately for her, one day when her son was playing in a garden he was bitten by a poisonous snake and he died. Her heart sank to the greatest depths of misery. Hearing the news of her son's death, she went mad. She refused to believe that her son was dead. Taking her dead son here and there she appealed to everybody that her son was in a deep sleep. Somebody should wake him up. But wherever she went people told her that he was dead and not sleeping. One day somebody sent her to Buddha who was staying at Jetavana Vihāra.

The Buddha understood her mental condition. In his unique style of teaching *Dhamma* depending on the mental condition of a person, the Buddha with a lot of compassion told her to bring a handful of mustard grains from a family where no one had died. Kisā Gotami walked throughout the day in the streets of Sāvatthi begging for a handful of mustard grains. People offered her bags

The Buddha teaching Dhamma to Kisā Gotami

of mustard grains. But when she asked them whether no one had died in their family, each one of them told countless stories of death of near and dear ones. By the evening, she must have visited hundreds of households only to find that death is a common fact of life. Totally tired but back in her senses, she returned to the Buddha and took refuge in the triple gems: the Buddha, the *Dhamma* and the *Saṅgha.* She realised the truth of impermanence. Leading a life of *Sīlā, Samādhi* and *Paññā,* she reached the stage of *Sotāpātti (*first stage of *nibbanic* bliss).[7]

Angulimālā

Angulimālā's original name was Ahimsaka (innocent) [8]. His father was the chaplain to the king of Kosala. He received his education at Taxila, the famous educational centre in the olden days, and became the most illustrious and favourite pupil of his renowned teacher. Unfortunately his colleagues grew jealous of him, concocted a false story, and succeeded in poisoning the teacher's mind against him. The enraged teacher, without any investigation, contrived to put an end to his life by ordering him to fetch a thousand human right- hand fingers as a teacher's honorarium. In obedience to the teacher, though with great reluctance, he went to the Jalini forest, in Kosala, and started killing people to collect fingers for the necessary offering. The fingers thus collected were hung on a tree, but as crows and vultures destroyed them, he later wore a garland of those fingers to ascertain the exact number. Hence he was known by the name Aṅgulimāla (finger-wreathed).

In the twentieth year of the Enlightenment, the Buddha was staying at Jetavana Vihāra. By then, Aṅgulimāla had already collected nine hundred and ninety nine fingers. The terror of Aṅgulimāla was such that not even soldiers dared to pass through the Jalini forest. People of the nearby areas lived in constant fear. There was suffering all around. With infinite compassion, the Buddha wanted to give relief to the suffering public. Therefore, the Buddha decided to teach the *Dhamma* to Aṅgulimāla. So, he went to the Jalini forest to meet Aṅgulimāla. Overjoyed at the sight, because he thought that he could complete the required number by killing the great ascetic, Aṅgulimāla stalked the Buddha drawing his sword. The Buddha by his psychic powers created obstacles on the way so that Aṅgulimāla would not be able to get near him although he walked at his usual pace. Aṅgulimāla ran as fast as he could but he could not overtake the Buddha. Panting and sweating, he stopped and cried: "Stop, ascetic." The Buddha calmly said: "Though I walk, yet have I stopped. You too, Aṅgulimāla stop."

Conversion of Aṅgulimāla

The bandit thought, 'These ascetics speak the truth, yet he says he has stopped, whereas it is I who have stopped'. Aṅgulimāla's good *Kamma* rushed up to the surface. He realized that the great ascetic was none other than the Lord Buddha who out of compassion had come to help him. Straightaway he threw away his armour and sword and took refuge in the triple gems and started practising *Dhamma.*

News spread that Aṅgulimāla had become a *bhikkhu*. The king of Kosala, in particular, was greatly relieved to hear of his conversion because he was a great source of danger to his subjects.

But venerable Aṅgulimāla had no peace of mind, because even in his solitary meditation he used to recall the memories of his past and the pathetic cries of his unfortunate victims. Due to his past actions, he would become a target for stray stones and sticks and he would return to the monastery with broken head and flowing blood, cut and crushed to be reminded by the Buddha that he was merely reaping the effects of his own *Kamma*.

One day as he went on his round for alms he saw a woman in pain unable to deliver her unborn child. Moved by compassion, he reported this pathetic woman's suffering to the Buddha. He then advised him to pronounce the following words of truth, which later came to be known as the *Aṅgulimāla Paritta.*

"Sister, since my birth in the Noble *Dhamma* (i.e. since his ordination) I have never intentionally harmed any living being. By that merit, may you and your child be peaceful and safe."

He studied this *Paritta* and, going to the presence of the suffering sister, sat on a seat separated from her by a screen, and uttered these words. Instantly she delivered a child with ease. The efficacy of this *Paritta* persists to this day. In due course venerable Aṅgulimāla attained Arahantship.

Referring to his memorable conversion by the Buddha, he said:

Some creatures are subdued by force,
Some by the hook, and some by whips,
But I by such a One was tamed,
Who needed neither staff nor sword.

Visākhā

Visākhā was the devout and generous daughter of millionaire Dhanañjaya. Her mother was Sumanā Devī, and her grandfather was the millionaire Meṇḍaka.

When she was only seven years old, she came in contact with the Buddha and attained the *Sotapātti* (first stage of sainthood). She was famous for her beauty and manners. At the age of sixteen, she was married to Puṇṇāvaddhana, son of a multimillionaire Migāra. He was a follower of Nigaṇṭha Nāṭaputta. One day, he invited a large number of naked ascetics to his house for alms. Visākhā was asked to pay homage to these naked ascetics. She refused. The naked ascetics took offence and found fault with the millionaire for having brought a female follower of the Buddha to his house. They asked him to expel her from the house immediately. Migāra pacified them by promising them not to offer alms to *Bhikkhus*. One day, when he was eating rice-porridge, a *Bhikkhu* entered the house for alms. Visākhā was fanning her father-in-law and without informing him of his presence she moved aside so that he might see him. Migāra ignored the *Bhikkhu* and continued eating as if he had not seen him.

Visākhā telling the monk that her father- in-law is eating stale food

Visākhā politely told the *Bhikkhu:* "Pass on, venerable Sir, my father-in-law is eating *purāṇaṁ* (stale food)."[9]

The ignorant millionaire, misconstruing her words, was so provoked that he ordered the bowl to be removed and Visākhā to be expelled from the house.

Visākhā asked to summon eight clansmen who were present at the time of marriage to ajudicate after investigating her guilt or innocence. Migāra agreed.

Visākhā politely told them that a *Bhikkhu* was standing at the door for alms, Migāra was eating sweet milk rice-porridge, ignoring him. Thinking to herself that her father-in-law, without performing any new good deeds in life, is only consuming the merits of past deeds *(puranam)*, she told the *Bhikkhu*: "Pass on, venerable Sir, my father-in-law is eating stale food." What fault of hers was there in this?

She was found not guilty. Having proved her innocence, self-respecting Visākhā now desired to leave the house as she was ordered to do so at first.

Migāra's attitude towards Visākhā was completely changed, and he was compelled to seek pardon from his daughter-in-law for what he had uttered through ignorance.

Forbearing Visākhā, in accordance with her true Buddhist spirit, granted him pardon on condition that he would give complete freedom to her to carry on her religious activities as she desired. Her father-in-law readily agreed to this and granted her full freedom to perform her religious activities. Visākhā, lost no time in inviting the Buddha to the house for alms. The Buddha came and had his meal. After the meal was over the Buddha preached the *Dhamma*. Migāra sat behind a curtain and listened to the Buddha. At the end of the discourse he became *Sotāpanna* and acknowledged his boundless gratitude to his daughter-in-law for having initiated him into the True Path of Deliverance and emotionally remarked that he would hereafter regard Visākhā as his mother. Therefore, Visākhā was known as Migāramātā Visākhā.

On the following day the Buddha visited her house, and on that occasion her mother-in-law heard the *Dhamma* and became a *Sotāpanna*.

By her tact, wisdom, and patience she gradually succeeded in converting her husband's household to a happy Buddhist home.

Visākhā used to give alms daily to the *Saṅgha* at her own house. Both in the forenoon and afternoon she used to visit the monastery to minister to the needs of the *Saṅgha* and hear sermons from the Buddha. Being a lady of many qualities, she played an important role in various activities connected with the Sāsana. At times she was deputed by the Buddha to settle disputes that arose amongst *Bhikkhunis*. Some *Vinaya* rules were also laid down for *Bhikkhus* owing to her intervention. Owing to her magnanimity she was regarded as the chief benefactress of the *Sāsana* and the greatest female supporter of the Buddha. By her dignified conduct, graceful deportment, refined manners, courteous speech, obedience and reverence to elders, compassion to those who were less fortunate, kind hospitality, and religious zeal, she won the hearts of all who knew her. She died at the ripe age of one hundred and twenty.

Opponents of the Buddha

Ciñcā

The followers of the Buddha were increasing day by day. He brought a social revolution by opening the door of Saṅgha to all sections of the society irrespective of caste, creed, gender and economic status. His teachings were simple. Therefore, millions and millions of people in North India became his followers. His followers stopped superstitious y*ajanas*, which adversely affected the income of the priestly class. Therefore, they conspired to discredit him in the eyes of the common man.[10] Since he renunciated the life of a prince, they could not allege corruption against him. Therefore, they used a young and beautiful Brāhmanī *Parivrājikā* known as Ciñcā in their plot against the Buddha. Ciñcā used to go to Jetavana in the evening and spent the night under some tree and return in the morning uttering words that she had a nice stay during the night. After a few days she disappeared and resurfaced after nine months with a piece of wood fastened around her stomach. She went to the gathering where Lord Buddha was teaching *Dhamma* and shouted in the presence of a number of followers that Gotama should at least care for his son, which she was carrying. Everybody was shocked. Had the Buddha wanted he could have asked the king Pasenadi to chop off Ciñcā's head for the baseless allegation. But he smiled and with infinite compassion said: "Sister, whatever you have said, whether true or false, is only known to us both." Ciñcā coughing loudly, said. "Yes, O Teacher, such a thing can be known to us only." With her coughing, the knot with which the wooden protuberance was tied round her belly slackened, and it fell on her feet to her discomfiture. She was turned away with stones and sticks. The conspirators must have thought that the Buddha would react to the false allegations with anger and they would reply with more anger and create a scene and involve the Buddha in a war of nerves. But they were not

Ciñcā making false allegations

prepared for the smile and infinite compassion of the Buddha. The compassionate response of the Buddha must have made Ciñcā nervous and she coughed, which loosened the knots of the wooden protuberance.

Devadatta

Devadatta was a cousin of Gotama the Buddha. He entered the *Bhikkhu Saṅgha* in the early part of the Buddha's ministry together with Ānanda and other Śākya princes. He could not attain any of the stages of sainthood, but was distinguished for worldly psychic powers (*pothujjanika-iddhi*).[11]

During the early part of his career he led an exemplary life.

Later, overcome by worldly gain and honour, and growing jealous of the Buddha, Devadatta became so radically changed in his character that he proved to be the greatest personal enemy of the Buddha. Simultaneous with the arising of ill-will in his heart towards the Buddha, his psychic powers automatically ceased. He requested the Buddha to hand over the leadership of the Saṅgha to him as the Buddha was advanced in age. The Buddha refused. Devadatta was enraged at this refusal and vowed vengeance. To safeguard and maintain the dignity of the *Saṅgha* the Buddha caused a proclamation to be made that Devadatta alone was responsible for anything done by him in the name of the Buddha, the *Dhamma,* or the *Saṅgha.*

Devadatta conspired with prince Ajātasatru to kill the Buddha. Ajātasatru was advised to kill his father and usurp the throne while he himself decided to kill the Buddha and lead the *Saṅgha*. An ungrateful Ajātasatru succeeded in killing his devout father, and Devadatta hired bowmen to assasinate the Buddha but, contrary to his expectations, all the hirelings became the Buddha's followers. Foiled in his attempt, he himself resolved to kill the Buddha. When the Buddha was walking on the slopes of Gijjhakūṭa (Vulture's Peak) he climbed the Peak and mercilessly hurled a rock at the Buddha. Fortunately it struck another piece of rock and a splinter slightly wounded the Buddha's foot, causing the blood to flow. Devadatta made another unsuccessful attempt to kill the Buddha by dispatching the elephant Nālāgiri, after infuriating him with liquor, against the Buddha. When the ferocious elephant approached the Buddha the venerable Ānanda stepped forward to sacrifice his life for the sake of his Master, but the Buddha subdued the elephant by his loving-kindness (*Metta*).

By this last wicked act, Devadatta became extremely unpopular, and public opinion was so much against him that the king was compelled to withdraw his patronage. Devadatta fell into disrepute and all his favours decreased. He now decided to live by deceit. His fertile brain devised another seemingly peaceful plan. With the help of equally evil- minded *Bhikkhus* like Kokālika, he thought of causing a schism in the *Saṅgha.*

He requested the Buddha to enforce the following five rules among the Bhikkhus:

The Subjugation of Nālāgiri, Amarāvatī

i. That the monks should dwell all their lives in the forest.
ii. That they should live on alms begged.
iii. That they should wear *Paṁsukula* robes (robes made from rags collected from the dust heap and cemeteries).
iv. That they should live at the foot of a tree.
v. That they should not eat fish or flesh throughout life.

The Buddha refused to make the above rules compulsory. Devadatta made this refusal a cause for a schism in the *Saṅgha*. He gathered about five hundred monks and took them to Gayāshīrœa. But venerable Sāriputta and Mogallāyana brought back about four hundred *Bhikkhus*. Thereafter evil days fell upon Devadatta. He fell grievously ill, and before his death he sincerely repented. He had to die a miserable death. However, he sought refuge in the

Buddha at the last moment.

The Buddha preached on all subjects relating to human life like relationship in the family and in the society, income and expenditure, democracy, equality, defence and ultimate liberation from the cycle of birth and death. Some of his views are given below:

Dhamma for Householders

Preaching the *Dhamma* to the householders, the Buddha explained that the lay disciples could also walk on the path of *Dhamma* and achieve true happiness. He preached that the desire for wealth should not overpower so much that one cannot give happiness to oneself and his family. Living in the present moment of happiness is most important. He explained that a look filled with understanding, a simple smile, a loving word, a meal shared in warmth and awareness are the things which create happiness in the present moment. By cultivating awarness in the present moment, one could avoid causing suffering to oneself and those around him. The way one looks at others, one's smile and one's small acts of caring could create happiness. True happiness does not depend on wealth or fame alone. In the *Sigālovāda Sutta*, the Buddha preached to Sigālo the duties towards parents, wife and children, coworkers and teachers. He explained the qualities of a good friend.

The Buddha said that we are immensely indebted to our parents for it is they who bring us into this world. They raise their children with lot of sacrifice and pain. We should treat parents as Brahmā. *"Brahmāti mātāpitoro"*– parents are real Brahmā. Even if one carries his parents on his shoulders throughout life, still they can not free themselves from their debt to their parents. The Buddha said that one cannot repay the debt of parents except in three circumstances. Firstly, if parents are not following five precepts in their life and they are persuaded and motivated to follow the precepts. Secondly, if they are living life of precepts but are not established in *Samādhi* (mastery over mind), then by persuading and motivating them to get established in Samādhi and thirdly, if they are living the life of *Sīlā* (morality) and *Samādhi* (mastery over mind) but are not established in *Paññā* (experiential wisdom), then by persuading and motivating them to get established in *Paññā.* In short, one can get absolved of duties towards parents only by establishing them in *Dhamma.*

The Buddha preached that it is the duty of all the parents to provide the best education to their children. They should keep them away from bad company, ensure good company, get them married at a proper age and into a suitable family. They should hand over the family reigns at the appropriate time.

The Buddha calls the relationship between wife and husband sacred love. They should be faithful to each other throughout their life. The Buddha preached equality of status between husband and wife. Husband and wife are equal and complementary to each other. No one is superior or inferior to the other. Each one performs his or her duty. A woman being manager of the house, 'wealth and honour of the house' has special responsibility in managing the household, and a husband being a *grihapati*, 'head of the family' is supposed to provide sufficient funds for the purpose. The prescribed duties of the husband and wife are as under:

The **husband's duties** to his wife are:

i. To treat his wife with respect
ii. To treat her with kindness
iii. To be faithful to her
iv. To keep her content by having adequate source of income
v. To provide her with ornaments and clothes

The **wife's duties** to her husband are:

i. To keep the management of her household in perfect order
ii. To keep all family members happy by good behaviour
iii. To be a faithful wife
iv. To be a thrifty housekeeper
vi. To show skill and diligence in discharging her duties

The Buddha prescribed the duties of teachers and students also. He says that it is the duty of the teacher to teach the students to the best of his or her capacity and ability and to impart the education to the students as per their aptitude and potential. The teacher should not discriminate between the students. He should guide them in choosing the right courses and right profession and should help them in finding employment. The students should respect the teacher all the time and be grateful towards the teacher throughout life.

The Buddha said that we should be good neighbours. We should help our neighbours in their hour of need. We should try to understand the problems of our neighbours and should help them even before they ask for our help.

The Buddha goes on to prescribe the duties of friendship. He says that a friend in need is a friend indeed. A friend should not speak ill of his friend before others. He or she should conceal his or her friend's bad qualities before others and should reveal only his or her good qualities before others. He should prevent him from treading the wrong path and should help in inculcating good qualities.

The Buddha preached that true happiness could be realized in this very life especially when one fosters relations with people of virtue and avoids the path of degradation; resides in an environment that is conducive to spiritual practice and builds good character; fosters opportunities to learn more about the *Dhamma,* the precepts, and one's own trade in greater depth; takes time to care well for one's own parents, spouse and children; shares time, resources, and happiness with others; fosters opportunities to cultivate virtues, avoids alcohol and gambling; cultivates humility, gratitude, and simple living; seeks opportunities to be close to *Bhikkhus* in order to study the *Dhamma*; lives a life based on the Four Noble Truths and learns how to meditate in order to release sorrows and anxieties.

Views on Income & Spending

The Buddha knew that economic stability is essential for man's material happiness. Therefore, he advised people to earn their livelihood to the best of their ability without intimidating others "like a roving bee that gathers honey without damaging flowers."[12]

He said: "Wealth should be acquired honestly, by energetic striving and sweat of brow."[13] He observed that in acquiring wealth one should not be deterred by cold, heat, flies, mosquitoes, wind, sun, creeping things, dying of hunger and thirst, but that one should be prepared to endure all these difficulties.[14] In earning money one is advised to be scrupulously ethical by abstaining from selling intoxicants, harmful weapons, drugs, poisons or animals to be killed or trading in flesh (which would include the slave trade). Such activities fall into the category of wrong livelihood.[15] One's livelihood has to be earned through lawful means, non-violently.[16]

The prescription for acquiring of wealth is followed up with ethical considerations. Directing attention to the development of moral qualities along with one's daily activities connected with earning money acts as a break to ever increasing greed. The purpose of restraining greed or sensual desires is to develop contentment with less wants. Being content with few wants is another principle extolled in Buddhism. The Buddha's famous piece of advice regarding how one should spend one's income is found in Dīgha Nikāya III (p.188). He suggests that one divide one's income into four portions. One portion should be spent on day-to-day expenses, two portions for investing in one's business or industry and the fourth portion kept in reserve for a rainy day. Even if in the context of modern economic life, which is far more complex than the comparatively simple monetary transactions that existed during the time of the Buddha in India, the general principle of his advice still holds good, though the portions may vary. The Buddha's advice on how one should spend wealth shows that he considers ethical values to be necessary not only with regard to earning money but spending it as well. One is advised to spend money by sharing it with one's family, employees, relatives, and friends and by making offerings to religious recluses.[17] Such a man, he says, could be compared to a lovely lake of clear, blue, cool water which lies near a village or township from which people can draw water, drink and bathe in [18].

It must be pointed out that the Buddha did not preach one kind of doctrine to the laity and another to *bhikkhus*. The ethical values he preached are universal.

The distinction between the two ways of life is the extent of restraint placed on the senses. For instance, when an individual takes the path of renunciation, there were certain traditional modes of conduct during the Buddha's time, which the renunciate had to adopt. A blanket term for such renunciates was '*Paribbājaka*' or

Bhikkhu and one of the principal modes of conduct for them was living on alms.

The distinction drawn between the two modes of life, therefore, was the emphasis on sense restraint. This is because the Buddha well understood the limitations placed on lay life in finding the 'space' required for the rigors of mind training which is all-important for disciplining of senses. Therefore, he urged the laity to follow the *pañcasīla* code of ethics and earn money not for its own sake but to fulfill duties and for one's own enjoyment within limits.

The Buddha and Gender Equality

The Buddha preached and practiced equality. He ordained mother and former wife of Yasa to be Upāsikā after the very first sermon delivered at the Deer Park, Isipatana. In the fifth year of his Enlightenment (524 B.C.), the Buddha ordained Mahāprajāpati Gotami, his step mother with her five hundred followers as nuns and founded the first monastic order of Nuns in the world history. The Buddha became the first teacher in the history of human civilization to allow ordination of women, which gave them an alternative to domesticity. Thousands of women became *Bhikkhunis* and the Buddha praised their spiritual attainment. The Buddha said that women are as capable as men to lead contemplative life and tread the path of Enlightenment. There is no gender distinction when we consider about the goal of human life. Every human being is endowed with the potential to become an *Arahata.*

The Buddha illustrated in the Tathāgata-garbha-sutta that all sentient beings are endowed with the Buddha nature without exception. There is no discrimination between the male and female. Both genders are equally capable to achieve the perfect Enlightenment. Because they are both equally laden with a natural potential to bloom to the flower of Buddhahood, that is why both of them are naturally gifted with the seed of the Buddha, which lives in the inner core of the mind-stream.

In the ocean of *Saṁsāra*, chances of women swimming across to the further shore were as good as those of man. Emancipation of the mind through perfection of wisdom which is referred to as *Cetovimutti, Paññāvimutti* was the goal of spiritual life and for this the way which had proved most effective was the life of renunciation (*agārasmā anagāriyam pabbajjā*). The woman was as encumbered by household life as man and in her spiritual earnestness she would have equally well echoed the words of the man who chooses renunciation. She would say with him that domestic life is full of impediments and contrast it with the life of *Pabbajjā*.

What was new and significant about the Buddha's teachings was that the women could attain *arahathood* and they could do so by following the same path as men. Certain limitations were made on the social equality of *Bhikkhus* and *Bhikkhunis*, and these limitations were probably made in order to increase societal acceptance of the monastic orders.

The Buddha raised the status of women and brought them to a realization of their importance in the society. Before the advent of the Buddha, women were not held in high esteem. But the Buddha gave them an honourable place in the order. 'He recognized the political right of the woman to join the *Saṅgha,* become the leader, develop her own personality and individuality, independent of any male support. The Buddha broke the myth of family and the importance of producing male children to attain salvation. He was the first to recognize the need for women's education and political initiative.'[19] Their admission into Saṅgha liberated them form household drudgery. The Buddha broke the firm shackle of the pervasive social norms in which there was unjust and unbelievable discrimination between the male and female. No wonder, therefore, that some authors recognized the Buddha as the first feminist in the world.

Several women contemporaries of the Buddha treated the establishment of the *Bhikkhuni Saṅgha* as a new opportunity to improve their status. The *Bhikkhunis* inspired vast sections of women. Hundreds and thousands of women were influenced by the Buddha's teachings. A number of them like Khemā, Uppalavaṇṇā, Sumaṅgalā, *Mathika*, Vāsanti and Sumedhā among others, became very well known in the Saṅgha and also in the wider world. 'The Buddha believed that women also can attain knowledge and through knowledge *nibbāna*.'[20] Throughout history we hardly come across movements, which provided women with such an opportunity. The steps that the Buddha had taken were unique. The fact that courtesans were admitted into the *Saṅgha* was a clear indication of his sympathetic understanding of women's problems and his firm belief in gender equality.

In this order of the nuns, queens, princesses, daughters of noble families, widows, bereaved mothers, helpless women, courtesans all irrespective of their caste or rank met on a common footing, enjoyed perfect consolation and place, and breathed in a free atmosphere which was denied to those confined in cottages and palatial mansions. Many women, who otherwise would have fallen into oblivion, distinguished themselves in various ways and gained their emancipation by seeking refuge in the Buddhist order. [21]

In the order of nuns, women were freely permitted to have ordination. They could stay in the nunnery and make spiritual progress. These women were entitled to have equal status with men. These women could not be treated inferior to man in any way as far spiritual path was concerned. Therefore, I.B. Horn says, "What the Buddha did for women shines as a bright light in the history of freedom. It brought its own rewards, not fugitive but lasting."

The Buddha allowed political freedom to women and in the process provided them political education as a part of *Saṅgha* life. He gave them the scope for literary and cultural development. Therigāthā, which was written by the Buddhist nuns, gives a clear picture of their talent and political acumen.[22] When they compare their physical appearance in their youth and old age their expression combines poetic and aesthetic talent. After Subhā (a Buddhist nun) joined the *Saṅgha* her faculties were developed and then she was freed from all ties. This kind of self-assessment is not possible unless the person concerned is highly conscious, and such consciousness could not have developed unless there was a systematic educative process at work in *Saṅgha* life, one which nurtured the individual personality. The Buddha departed radically from Vedic practice in admitting women to the *Saṅgha*, in allowing them to take political initiative, and in breaking the myth of family and marriage.

Some authors have contended that the Buddha was against the women joining his order. However, on being persuaded by Ānanda he allowed the women to join the Order, but told Ānanda that the *Dhamma* which otherwise would have survived one thousand years, would now survive for five hundred years only.

This does not appear to be correct and appears to be a mischievous interpolation. First of all the Buddha was a champion of equality for women. He was the first in the history of human civilization to allow ordination of women, which gave them an alternative to domesticity. Thousands of women became *bhikkhunis* and the Buddha praised their spiritual attainment. The *Bhikkhuni Saṅgha* of nuns he founded flourished in Sri Lanka until about the Cholian invasion of Anurādhapura in AD 1017, after which it dwindled and withered away due to adverse circumstances. But it was again revived in 1996. Secondly, had the Buddha really said so, then how could the *Dhamma* have survived in other countries like China, Taiwan, Vietnam, Japan, Burma, Bhutan, Sri Lanka, Korea and Cambodia?

The hostile attitude to women both in spiritual matters and in society was repeatedly criticized and challenged by the Buddha on numerous occasions. He had a high regard for women. In the Kosala Saṁyutta, the Buddha rejected the belief that the birth of a daughter was not as much a cause of joy as that of a son. The Buddha pointed out very clearly that the woman had a dignified and an important part to play in the society, and he defined her role with great insight, fitting her harmoniously into the social fabric. She is a loveable member of the household, held in place by numerous relationships, and respected above all as the mother of worthy children. The gender did not matter, he argued, and added that in character and in her role in society, she may even rival men.

The Buddha was once staying at Anāthapiṇḍika's Jetavanārāma in Shrāvasti. One day the king of the Kosalas, Pasendi had come to visit him. While the king was engaged in a conversation with the Buddha, a messenger from the palace arrived and approaching the king, informed him that queen Mallikā had given birth to a daughter. The king appeared to be very sad. The Buddha asked the king the reason for his sadness. The king replied that he had just received the news that queen Mallikā had given birth to a daughter.

Understanding the matter, the Buddha explained to the king

the importance of daughter and gender equality and said:

'A woman child, O lord of men, may prove even a better offspring than a male. For she may grow up wise and virtuous, her husband's mother reverencing true wife, a daughter. The boy that she may bear may do great deeds and rule great realms, yea, such a son of a noble wife becomes his country's guide".

In the modern world when people in some developing countries are resorting to female foeticide the above teaching of the Buddha becomes all the more relevant.

The instances are numerous where the Buddha defines and ascribes the duties of women in society. The Buddha recognizes the fact that these by no means constitute the whole of her life. It is not with a view to limiting their life solely to the secular affairs of the household that the Buddha laid down a code of good living for women, but to serve as a complement to the good life already enjoined in his order to all his followers, irrespective of their gender. A host of these considerations as they are addressed to women are grouped together in the *Saṁyutta Nikāya* in a chapter solely devoted to them as *Mātugāma Saṁyutta*.

The Buddha and Social Equality

The social organizations, which the Buddha took upon himself directly to set up and mould was the *Saṅgha* which was far from being organized along mercenary lines. But, at the same time the Buddha did not hold that moral perfection is a monopoly of the *Saṅgha*. His true spiritual disciples, the *Sāvaka Saṅgha*, existed both among the monastic order and the laity.

The central theme of Buddhism is to recognise that all human beings are equal and that caste distinctions are inhuman. The prevalence of the caste system, which denigrates and discriminates among the lower castes, by the assumed superiority of the dominant caste, is unacceptable to the intelligensia. Buddhist teachings of the practice of non- discrimination is appealing to people, as it provides them with self-esteem and personal dignity – basic psychological needs of all human beings.

The subalternised masses found in the Buddha and his teachings a haven from their socio-cultural degradation and economic and political deprivation. For them, Buddhism came as a vehicle to emerge into a new and modern religio cultural, and eventually socio political, reality. We must realize that *Nibbāna* is to be attained by our own personal endeavour and that it is not a paradise to which a Buddha can carry us. Buddhas are powerful, more powerful by far than any other living beings. But this is something even Buddhas cannot do. Each being must work out its own salvation.

Prior to the advent of the Buddha, India was unaware of the ethics of equality and universal brotherhood. The society based on the *Caturvarṇa* was regulated by the principle of graded inequality; the *Brahmins* being at the top followed by *Kshatriyas, Vaishyas* and *sudras* in a descending order. This rule of graded inequality regulated their rights and privileges as well. Even the punishments for secular offences were based on the principle of inequality; the Brahmins always getting the minimum and the shudras the maximum punishment.

The Buddha revolted against such oppressive social laws and condemned the caste system. He challenged the divine origin of the caste, and showed the hollowness of the claim of the Brahmins of having been born from the mouth of Brahma. He also refuted the Brahmins' claim that only they could attain spiritual virtues, and asserted that a person of any caste, colour, creed or gender can develop in his heart such virtues. He further said: "Let no person, whether man or woman, whatever be his or her socio economic background, be hindered from reaching the highest perfection, which is every one's right, and within every one's reach and more than that is achievable by the dint of one's own ceaseless striving."

The Buddha further pointed that all human beings were alike and to divide them artificially was folly. He said that in the case of animal life there are different species based on different characteristics. So is the case with the plant life. But there do not exist such differences which justify classification of human beings. Human beings are one and the same in their essential characteristics. The Buddha also took concrete steps to eradicate the evil of caste. These steps exposed the fallacies of the myth of hereditary superiority claimed by certain castes; encouraging the downtrodden by dining at their houses; and accepting the low and lowly as equal members of the *Saṅgha*. Exhorting the *Bhikkhus* to forget their caste labels, the Buddha said:

> *"Just O brethren, as the great rivers—Gangā, Yamunā, Acīravatī, Saraswati and Mahī-loose their different names and are known as the great ocean, just so, O brethren, do these four castes—when they begin to follow the doctrine and discipline as propounded by the Tathāgata, they renounce different names of castes and ranks and become members of one and the same society."*

The Buddha's followers came from all strata of society. They include Upāli, who had been a barber, and who became an authority on the Vinaya and led the recitation of it at the First Council.

There were people like Nanda, the cowherd of Kosambi; Yasoja, headman of the fishermen of a fishing village; Bhalliya, son of a caravan driver; Suppiya of the clan of watchmen in a cemetery; Sumaṅgala, a poor farmer; Sunita, a scavenger; Isidatta, son of a caravan guide; Vijitasena, an elephant trainer's son; Tālaputta, director of a company of actors and numerous poor people like Jambuka, Sopāka, Ajina and also Kappata Kura who used to go before in rags begging for grains of rice. All these people achieved the highest moral goal, ethical perfection. Cunda who gave the Buddha his last meal was a metal worker. Among them, those who reached the highest and who came from the poor section of society were Kisā-gotami, Sumaṅgalā's mother who was a rush-weaver's wife, Puṇṇā the slave, Candā, the beggar woman and Cāpā, the deer trapper's daughter.

The Buddha touched the hearts and minds of millions of people by walking hundreds and hundreds of miles on foot up and down the valley of the Ganges for forty-five years preaching the *Dhamma* to all. It was for this very purpose, of taking the message to all and sundry that he sent his first sixty disciples in all directions and commanded them that each of them go alone.

The Buddha provided a powerful critique of the hierarchical caste structure in India, which perpetuated social inequalities. He infused ethical values into the existing social structures, institutions and forms of government. This is clearly seen in the advice given to the Vajji-s of the Vajji Republic in *Saptaṅgika Sutta*.

How to Defend the Country

The Buddha did not limit himself to teaching non-violence. He also preached self-defence and also how to defend the country from external aggressions.

The Buddha was once staying in Rājagraha, on the hill called the Vultures' Peak. The king of Magadha Ajātasatru was expanding his kingdom and wanted to attack the Vajjins. He sent his prime minister Vassakāra to the Buddha to take his advice in the matter. Accordingly Vassakāra went to vultures peak and after saluting the Buddha, he delivered the message as the king had commanded.

The venerable Ānanda was standing behind the Buddha. The Buddha asked him: "Have you heard, Ānanda, that the Vajjins hold full and frequent public assemblies? "Lord, so I heard," replied Ānanda.

"So long, Ānanda," rejoined the Buddha, "as the Vajjins hold these full and frequent public assemblies; so long may they be expected not to decline, but to prosper.

"So long, Ānanda, as the Vajjins meet together in concord, and rise in concord, and carry out their undertakings in concord.

"So long as they enact nothing not already established, abrogate nothing that has been already enacted and act in accordance with the ancient institutions of the Vajjins as established in former days.

"So long as they honour and esteem and revere and support the Vajjin Elders, and make it a point of duty to listen to their words.

"So long as no women or girls belonging to their clans are detained among them by force or abduction.

"So long as the Vajjins respect and follow religion.

"So long, Ānanda, the Vajjins may be expected not to decline but to prosper and no one can destroy them."

In short, the Buddha declared that so long as the Vajjins believed in democracy and practiced democracy, there was no danger to their kingdom. Then the Buddha addressed Vassakāra and said: "When I was once staying at Vaishāli I taught the Vajjins these conditions of welfare."

"We may expect then," answered the prime minister, "the

welfare and not the decline of the Vajjins, so long as they observe these conditions. So, the Vajjins cannot be overcome by the king of Magadha." Vassakāra heard the words of the Buddha and went back to Rājagraha to inform the king of what the Buddha had said.

The above teachings of the Buddha are relevant for every country. The above teachings given to the Vajjins are helpful in promoting unity amongst citizens and national integration. They strengthen internal security by removing misgivings amongst citizens. They promote peaceful co-existence and mutual respect for each other. The Buddha also never taught surrender before injustice. For self-defence and protection of life and liberty of citizens, use of force was justified.

Democracy

The Buddha stressed a total commitment to democratic practices, which underpinned their constitution. He pointed out that the laws and customs of their people should be adhered to by the government of the day and if they wished to change them or pass new ones the legislature should introduce them and ratify them constitutionally in their state assembly according to procedures already laid down. He also urged lawmakers to be united and sincere to one another and not cause distrust among themselves.

The democratic procedures introduced into the conduct of affairs in the *Saṅgha* are noteworthy. They presage the rise of democracy in Great Britain, for instance, by at least two millennia. The *Saṅgha* was organized and managed strictly as per democratic principles. For bringing any change in the *Saṅgha,* a proper resolution was moved, debated and adopted by the voice vote. The rules were equally applicable to all the members of the *Saṅgha* irrespective of their seniority or status in the *Saṅgha*. The Saṅgha was governed by rule of the law as no one was above the rules of the *Saṅgha,* not even the Buddha himself. No member, howsoever senior he may be had any arbitrary powers. The administration of the *Saṅgha* was run strictly as per the laid down rules. The Buddha's language policy is another feature, which reflects his innate egalitarian outlook. He delivered all his sermons in the local language, *Pāli*.

The Buddha on Poverty Alleviation

The Buddha's ideas on poverty alleviation are contained in *Kuṭadanta-sutta*.

Addressing his followers at village Ālavi, the Buddha explained that 'there is no greater suffering than hunger'.[23] Hunger creates havoc and destroys human bodies, well-being, peace and joy. People should never forget those who are hungry. It is a discomfort to miss one meal, but think of the suffering of those who have not had a proper meal in days or even weeks. Ways and means must be found to ensure that no body in this world is forced to go hungry. The Buddha emphasized that no one should go without food. He was in favour of establishing an egalitarian society and equitable distribution of resources of the country so that there was no poverty. The islands of prosperity cannot survive for long if surrounded by the ocean of poverty. It is, therefore, in the interest of the entire country that ways and means must be found for equitable distribution of economic resources in such a way that no one remains without food.

Economic Development and Law & Order

The Buddha preached the king Pasenadi of Kosala to reform the system of justice and economy in the country. He told the King that capital punishment, torture and imprisonment cannot stop crime. Crime and violence are the natural result of unemployment, poverty and hunger. The best way to help the people and to ensure security was to build a healthy economy. It was essential to provide agricultural inputs to poor farmers until they could become self reliant. Credit facilities should be provided to small traders, the retired people should be given pensions and the poor should be exempted from taxes. All sorts of coercion and oppression against labourers and workers must stop. People should be free to choose their profession and jobs. People should be provided adequate training so that they can master the profession they choose. The economic policy should ensure people's voluntary participation.

He advised politicians to set an example of simplicity and not to live in luxury because it creates a barrier between the rulers and the people. Those in power should live a simple, wholesome life, using their time to serve the people, rather than pursuing idle pleasures. A leader cannot earn the trust and respect of his people if he does not set a good example. If the leader loves and respects the people, they will maintain the law and order. Rule by virtue differs from rule by law and order. Rule by virtue does not depend on punishment. According to the Way of Awakening, the path of virtue can only lead to true happiness.

The Buddha's means of persuading people to adopt the principles were by persuasion, by moral teaching and by love. He conquered the opponent by inculcating in him the doctrine that love and not power could conquer anything. The greatest thing that the Buddha taught was that the world cannot be reformed except by the reformation of the mind of the man, and the mind of the world. If the mind is changed, it does not require a soldier or a police officer to keep a man in order. It is because the Buddha energized people's conscience itself to purify their mind from defilement in order to keep them on the path of *Dhamma.*

The five precepts were the foundation of a happy family and a peaceful society. He explained that if politicians want the people to be united, they must first obtain their faith and trust. If political leaders practice the five precepts, the people's faith and trust will grow. With that faith and trust, there is nothing the country can't accomplish. Peace, happiness, and social equality will follow automatically. The leaders should create a life based on awareness. The dogmas of the past create barriers for equality among the people. The Way of Awakening offers a new path and a new faith. In today's world infested with terrorism and violence of every kind, the above preaching of the Buddha is much more relevant than any time earlier.

The Buddha and Communal Harmony

The Buddha was very well aware that the world is full of diversity. This diversity has been created by nature itself in various forms. There are people of different nature and belief. It can never happen that all the people subscribe to the same ideas and belief. It is, therefore, necessary for peaceful co- existence that we should have mutual respect for other beliefs and thoughts. Preaching the *Brahmajāla-sutta* to the bhikkhus at Ambalaṭṭhika in Nālandā, the Buddha said:

> *Bhikkhus*, whenever you hear some one criticize or ridicule the Buddha or the *Dhamma,* do not give rise to feelings of anger, irritation, or indignation. Such feelings can only harm you. Whenever you hear someone praise the Buddha or the *Dhamma,* do not give rise to feelings of happiness, pleasure or satisfaction. That too will only harm you. The correct attitude is to examine the criticism to see what parts may be true and what parts are not true. Only by doing that you will have a chance to further your studies and make real progress. *Bhikkhus,* most people who praise the Buddha, *Dhamma* and *Saṅgha* possess only superficial understanding. They appreciate how the *Bhikkhus* lead chaste, simple, and serene lives, but they do not see beyond that. Those who have grasped the most subtle and profound depths of the *Dhamma* speak few words of praise. They understand the true wisdom of enlightenment. Such wisdom is profound, sublime, and marvelous. It transcends all ordinary thoughts and words.
>
> "*Bhikkhus*, there are countless philosophies, doctrines and theories in this world. People criticize each other and argue endlessly over these theories. According to my investigation, there are sixty-two main theories which underlie the thousands of philosophies and religious beliefs in the world, seen from the point of enlightenment and emancipation, all sixty-two of thse theories contain errors and create obstacles.
>
> *Bhikkhus,* all these beliefs and doctrines have arisen because people have been carried away by their perceptions and feelings. When mindfulness is not practiced, it is not possible to see the real nature of perceptions and full feelings. When one can penetrate the roots and see into the true nature of perceptions and feelings, one will see

> the impermanency and interdependency of all phenomena. One will no longer be caught in the net of desire, anxiety and fear or the net of the sixty-two false theories."[24]

In today's world when people are clashing with each other in the name of religion and countries are waging war against each other in the name of clash of civilizations, the above teachings of the Buddha are not only relevant but worth following in order to maintain communal harmony in the society and international peace.

Do not Depend on the Favour of Politicians and Bureaucrats

Once the Buddha was staying at Rājagraha in the bamboo grove in the squirrels' feeding ground.

At that time prince Ajātasatru was supporting Devadatta who had turned hostile to the Buddha. The prince had extended royal hospitality with all kinds of favour to Devadatta and his supporters.

Some Bhikkhus informed the Buddha about the political and administrative favours being given to Devadatta and his supporters.

Then the Buddha addressing the monks said: "Do ye not long for gains, favours and flattery from the kings. So long, brethren, as prince Ajātasatru thus supports Devadatta late and early, with five hundred carts, conveying therein food brought in five hundred cooking-pots, it is ruin, brethren, that may be expected of Devadatta, and not growth in good conditions.

> Just as if, brethren, one were to crumble liver on a mad dog's nose, the dog would only get the madder, even so, brethren, so long as prince Ajātasatru thus supports Devadatta it is ruin that may be expected of Devadatta, and not growth in good conditions. Thus terrible, brethren, are gains, favours, and flattery of the princes.
>
> They are a bitter painful hindrance to the attainment of the sure peace that passeth all.

Wherefore, brethren, thus must you train yourselves: 'When gains, favours and flattery befall us, we will reject them, and when they do befall us, we will reject them, and when they do befall us, they shall not lay hold of and be established in our hearts, and make us slaves of the prince." [25]

The above teaching of the Buddha serves as a reminder to *Dhamma* brothers who seek favours from politicians and bureaucrats. The Buddha advised his followers to tread the path of the *Dhamma* relentlessly without bothering about favours from the politicians and bureaucrats.

If the Top Functionaries are Righteous, the Public will also be Righteous

Once the Buddha addressing the *Bhikkhus* said:

"Brethren, during such time as kings are unrighteous their ministers and officers also become unrighteous. The ministers and officers, brethren, being unrighteous, priests and householders also become unrighteous. The priests and householders, brethren, being unrighteous, the town-folk and villagers become unrighteous.

But whenever, brethren, kings are righteous, then kings' ministers and officers also became righteous. Whenever kings' ministers and officers become righteous the priests and householders also become righteous. Whenever priests and householders become righteous, the town-folk and villagers also become righteous.

When kine are crossing, if the old bull swerves, they all go swerving, following his lead. So among men, if he who is reckoned chief walks crookedly, the others crooked go.

Similarly, the whole realm suffers when the king goes wrong. When kine are crossing, if the bull goes straight they all go straight because his course is straight. So among men, if he who's reckoned chief walks righteously, the others live righteously. The whole realm leads happy lives when kings are good."[26]

The above teaching of the Buddha is a reminder to top functionaries of the government that if real reform is to be made, beginning will have to be made from the top. At the same time it is the duty of every person to be righteous and law abiding.

The Buddha and World Peace

Preaching *Dhamma* at Sāvatthi to the King *Pasenadi* of Kosala, the Buddha explained that the prosperity and security of one nation should not depend on poverty and insecurity of other nations. The lasting peace and prosperity are possible only when nations join together in a common commitment to seek the welfare of all. If a ruler wants his country to enjoy peace and to prevent the young men of his country from losing their lives in the battlefield, he must help other countries to find peace. The economic and foreign policies must follow the path of compassion for true and lasting peace. At the same time when one loves and cares for his countrymen, he can also love and care for the people of other countries. The nations can enjoy peace and security without having to resort to violent methods such as imprisonment and persecution. A ruler who cultivates compassion does not need to depend on violent means.

In the present uni-polar world, where powerful nations are using strong arm tactics against smaller and economically and militarily less developed countries, the above teachings of the Buddha appear to be much more relevant. It serves as a reminder to those who want the security of their citizens at the cost of insecurity of the citizens of other countries.

Spiritual Revolution

Before the advent of the Buddha, the Vedic society believed in Varṇāshrama *Dharma*, which consists of four stages of a human being's life. The first stage is up to twenty five years of age called *Brahmacarya* or celibacy. In this stage, a person is required to acquire knowledge through study. The second stage from twenty-five years to fifty years of age is called *Gārhasthāshrama* or life of a householder. In this stage, he is required to fulfil the duties and responsibilities of a householder. The third stage from fifty one years to seventy five years is called *Vānaprastha*. In this stage the man is required to migrate to the forest along with his wife and live in a hermitage or hut and pursue a religious life. He is still in touch with his family and relatives and links are not severed. The fourth and the last stage from seventy five years onwards is that of *Sanyāsa*, that is, complete renunciation. In this stage, a person is supposed to fully renunciate the world and devote himself completely to spiritual attainment for attaining *Moksha,* that is, liberation. The *Sanyāsa* is treated as worldly death. One is supposed to severe all attachments and worldly links with family and relatives.

The Buddha taught that *Dhamma* should be followed from a young age itself. One need not wait to grow old to seventy-five years of age for treading the path of the *Dhamma.* Practice of the *Dhamma* is a continuous phenomenon. Those who practice the *Dhamma* while young, illuminate the world like a full moon free of clouds. The practice of *Dhamma* can be undertaken by the people of any age. Those who start early get more benefit than those who start late. To the Buddha, a householder can pursue the spiritual journey along side his family duties and responsibilities.

Since the spiritual path shown by the Buddha was free from dogmas and ritualism, it appealed to the masses and people took to the Buddha's teachings in very large numbers. The Buddha brought a silent spiritual revolution throughout India, which spread to other parts of the world in the subsequent days. No wonder we see a large chain of saints in later periods coming from householder lives. Saint Kabir, Guru Ravidas, Guru Nanak Dev and so on all lead household lives.

It is not what you eat that makes you Holy

Sometime a debate is raised regarding the effect of vegetarian and non-vegetarian food on the mental condition of a person.

Some people believe that those who eat vegetarian food are more spiritual than those eating non-vegetarian food. The Buddha did not subscribe to such a view.

There was once a Brahmin called Āmagandha who lived in the region of the Himālayas with his pupils. They ate neither fish nor flesh. Every year, they would come down from their hermitage in search of salt and acids. Villagers would receive them with honour and give them hospitality for four months.

Once, the Buddha with his monks visited the same village.

After hearing the *Dhamma,* the villagers became his followers. That year, when Āmagandha and his disciples came to the village as usual, they were not received with much enthusiasm.

Āmagandha was disappointed to hear that the Buddha did not forbid the consumption of flesh and fish. Intending to confirm the matter, he went to Jeta Vana at Shrāvasti where the Buddha was then staying, and voiced his opinion: "Millet, *cingula*-beans and peas, edible leaves and roots, the fruit of any creeper – all these, obtained justly, are the food of the righteous. The eating of carrion is bad."

To this, the Buddha replied that though Āmagandha claimed to touch no carrion, he did consume choice dishes prepared with bird flesh, when they were given to him by others – and asked him the nature of his "carrion"

The Buddha emphasized:

> It is the useless taking of life, beating, cutting, binding, stealing, lying, fraud, deceiving, worthless knowledge and adultery; this is real carrion, not consumption of flesh.
>
> In this world, those individuals who are unrestrained in sensual pleasures, gluttonous, associated with unclean actions, who are of Nihilistic views, crooked and difficult to follow, are consumers of 'carrion' not non- vegetarians.
>
> In this world, those who are rude, harsh, treacherous, betrayers, unkind, excessively egoistic, ungenerous, and stingy are those who consume 'carrion', not non-vegetarians.
>
> Anger, pride, obstinacy, antagonism, deceit, envy, bluster, excessive egoism, association with the unrighteous; these are true carrion, not flesh or meat.
>
> It is those who are of bad morals, those who refuse to pay their debt, slanderers, deceitful in their dealings, pretenders, those who in this world being the vilest of men, commit such wrongdoings; this is carrion, Āmagandha, and not the eating of flesh.

> Those persons who, in this world, are uncontrolled towards living beings, who are bent on injuring others, having taken their belongings; immoral, cruel, harsh, disrespectful; this is carrion, Āmagandha, and not the eating of flesh.
>
> Those who attack these living beings either because of greed or of hostility, and always bent upon (evil), they go to darkness after death and fall into hell headlong; this is carrion, Amagandha, and not the eating of flesh.
>
> Abstaining from fish or flesh, nakedness, shaving of the head, matted hair, covering with ashes, wearing rough deer skins, attending the sacrificial fire, nor all these various penances in the world (performed) for immortality, neither incantations, oblations, sacrifices nor seasonal observances, purifies a person who has not overcome his doubt. [27]

Thus, it can be seen from the above that what the Buddha emphasized was sense-restrain, moral values and purification of mind. The dietary pattern is not of much significance when it comes to treading the path of spiritual attainment.

The life of the Buddha was a normal and natural life of a human being. He was born like a normal child. His childhood was normal and he married like a normal person and spent married life for thirteen years. He had a son and became a normal father. Gotama, the Buddha left worldly life for the welfare of mankind. He lived a very simple life and practiced morality. He preached what he practiced and he practiced what he preached (*yathāvādī tathākārī, yathākarī tathāvādī*). All the events relating to his life like birth, education, marriage, family life, enlightenment, his teachings and his passing away were historical events, which had been well documented. There was no myth and no mythology about his life.

Why the Buddha is called Lord Buddha or Bhagwan Buddha

The Buddha denied the existence of any creator god of this

universe and did not believe in the existence of soul. Referring to this some people frequently raise an argument that calling Buddha as 'Bhagwāna Buddha' or Lord Buddha' is against his teachings.

Prefixing 'Bhagawāna or Lord' with Buddha is not contrary to the teachings of the Buddha. He is not called 'Bhagawāna Buddha' or 'Lord Buddha' in the sense of creator. He is 'Bhagawāna' in the sense of one who has fully purified his mind from the defilements of craving, aversion and attachment. *'Pāli'* was the popular language during those time. In Pāli language 'Bhagawāna' means the one who has fully purified his mind from the defilements of craving, aversion and attachment. The *Pāli Sutta* says '*Bhagawāti Gāravādivacanaṁ'* which means the word 'Bhagwan' is a synonym of honour and dignity. Because of honour and dignity, he was called Bhagawāna. The word *Bhagga* means removed. It further says *'Bhaggarāgoti Bhagawā, Bhaggadosoti Bhagawā, Bhaggamohoti Bhagawā'.* Thus, the one who has completely removed all the defilements of craving, aversion and attachment came to be known as Bhagawāna. Therefore, the concept of Bhagawāna in Buddhist tradition is an achievement. It is a degree, which anybody can achieve by walking on the path shown by the Buddha. Therefore, it is said that every human being is a potential Buddha, and thus a potential Bhagwan.

The Buddha taught the *Dhamma* for forty-five long years without any discrimination based on caste, creed, gender and status in the society. The Buddha was the first in the world to grant religious equality to women and the deprived persons by admitting them in his order. He was the first missionary who sent his monks and nuns in all directions to teach the *Dhamma* for the welfare of all beings.

His teachings are much more relevant today as people suffer due to violence, terrorism, poverty and unemployment.

Sabba-pāpassa akaraṇaṁ, Kusalassa upasampadā, Sa-citta-pariyodapanaṁ, Etaṁ Buddhāna Sāsanaṁ.

(Abstain from all unwholesome deeds, perform wholesome ones, Purify your mind – this is the teaching of the enlightened persons)

Chapter 3
The Essence of Dhamma

The Buddha means the 'enlightened one' or the 'exalted one'. Any person, who walks on the path of *Dhamma* shown by the Buddha and fully purifies his mind from craving, aversion and attachment becomes enlightened. The Buddha has repeatedly said that he is only a guide and not a liberator. Every person has to liberate himself. Every person seeking cessation of suffering has to work out his own salvation.[1] No power in the universe can liberate a person unless the person himself walks on the path of *Dhamma*. The Buddha is also known as Tathāgata. Tathāgata means one who realizes the ultimate truth by walking on the path of *Dhamma* step-by-step. Tathāgata also means 'one who thus comes or one who thus goes'. [2] Any person who walks on this path can become Tathāgata and experience the *nibbanic* peace. The godhood, *Arahata*, *Mahāsthvira,* all these are states of mind. As the mind becomes purer and purer, one achieves higher and higher stages of liberation from the defilements of craving and aversion. He generates love, peace, compassion, friendship, fraternity, forgiveness and equanimity towards all beings. The Buddha taught the path to achieve the highest bliss by perfecting ten *Pāramis* or virtues or merits [3] viz:

1. *Dāna* (virtue in alms-giving)
2. *Silā* (morality)
3. *Nekkhamma* (renunciation)
4. *Paññā* (wisdom)
5. *Viriya* (perseverance)
6. *Khāṇti* (forbearance)
7. *Sacca* (truthfulness)
8. *Adhiṭṭhāna* (determination)

9. *Metta* (all embracing love)
10. *Upekkhā* (equanimity)

Morality, mastery over mind and direct experiential wisdom are the essence of the Buddha's teachings. Human beings and their welfare are the main concerns of the Buddha's teachings. He was interested in making human beings happy as only happy human beings can create a happy society. Human beings can become happy only when suffering ceases. He realized that human beings suffer due to various reasons like poverty, hunger, ignorance, disease, old age, death, unpleasant/unwanted events/ situations, non-happening of desired events/situations, separation from loved ones, meeting those whom we don't like.

The Buddha discovered that the root cause of all suffering is ignorance about the real nature of things. He discovered that whenever people face unwanted/undesirable situations or events, unpleasant sensations are generated in the body. Similarly, whenever desirable/wanted events/situations occur, pleasant sensations are generated. The unconscious mind generates craving for pleasant sensations and aversion against unpleasant sensations. People go on multiplying these craving and aversions, which generate deep-rooted *saṅkhāras*, which are the root cause of their miseries. The Buddha discovered the Four Noble Truths and the Eightfold Noble Path, which lead to cessation of suffering.

The discovery that the real cause of craving lies in sensation is the unparalleled gift of the Buddha to humanity. With this discovery, he gave us the key to open the door of liberation within ourselves. Others proclaimed that the six sensory organs cause craving *(salāyatana paccayā taṇhā),* the Buddha discovered and disclosed that sensations in the body cause craving *(vedanā paccayā taṇha*) which means that defilements arise at the sub-conscious level and in response to sensation (*vedanā*). If craving and aversion (*taṅhā*) arise due to sensation, any endeavour to reach the root of craving and aversion and to eradicate them must include the understanding of sensation, its experience and the knowledge of how it causes craving and aversion, and the wisdom to know how it can be used for the eradication of *taṅhā*.

Samāhito sampajāno, sato Buddhassa sāvako;
Vedanā ca pajānāti, vedananañca sambhavaṁ.
Yattha ceta nirujjhanti, maggañca khayagāminaṁ;
Vedanānaṁ khaya bhikkhu, niccato parinibbuto ti. [4]

Follower of the Buddha, with concentration, awareness and constant thorough understanding of impermanence, knows with wisdom the sensations, their arising, their cessation and the path leading to their end. A meditator who has reached the end (has experienced the entire range) of sensations (and has gone beyond) is freed from craving, is fully liberated.

The behaviour pattern of the mind is formed in the darkness of ignorance where one keeps reacting with craving and aversion, knowingly or unknowingly, towards bodily sensations. Thus, one becomes a slave of one's behaviour pattern and keeps reacting to sensations at the deepest level. The '*anusaya kilesa*' are sleeping volcanoes, the latent behaviour patterns, of blind reaction to sensations. The Buddha's discovery helps a meditator to come out of this blind behaviour pattern.

Among the many meditation techniques of India and other parts of the world, there is none that goes to the root cause of the defilements of craving and aversion and eradicates them. In no other technique is the way to eradicate even the latent tendencies of craving, aversion and ignorance so clearly spelled out:

Sukhāya, bhikkhave, vedanāya rāgānusayo pahātabbo, dukkhāya vedanāya paṭighānusayo pahātabbo, adukkhamasukhāya vedanāya avijjānusayo pahātabbo.[5]

(Eradicate the latent tendency of craving using pleasant sensations by equanimous observation of the pleasant sensations understanding their changing nature, eradicate latent tendency of aversion using unpleasant sensations and eradicate the latent tendency of ignorance using neutral sensations.) This is a unique contribution by the Buddha to humanity.

The path shown by the Buddha is based on equality. No person enjoys a high or low status on the basis of birth, caste, gender, financial status, place of birth. All the Buddhists have only one identity: that of following the path shown by the Buddha.

The Buddha preached the *Bhikkhus* saying that as all the rivers loose their identity when they meet the ocean and become part of ocean, similarly all the Dhammists when they follow the path of *Dhamma,* become part of his order and loose their individual identity of birth, caste, gender, financial status, place of birth.

Dhamma is a purely scientific way of life

Dhamma as a system is comparable to a scientific endeavour. It is a system for life and living in a world which is circumscribed with difficulty and beset with suffering. Science is based most assuredly on analysis, that is, the scrutinizing of every phenomena and examining every part of it and finding out how it came about. That is exactly what the Buddha did.

The assumption that there is pain, sorrow and misery, and the assumption that everything, no matter what has a cause, are the only two assumptions that the Buddha made. 'One is based on observation, introspection and a generalization from human experience; the other is the very life-blood of science, whether made in the East or in the West.' [6] By using a scientific method, the Buddha proved that he was, indeed, a scientist. He and his followers, and the whole procedure that the Buddhists employ, were and are in conformity with and in the spirit of science.

The Buddha and Buddhists welcome each scientific discovery, each new application of scientific principles, for these could never be contrary to the principles that they themselves employ. The Buddhists have greater concern with peace of mind, loving kindness towards all beings, *metta*, compassion, *karuṇā*, and a genuine interest in the joys of others, *muditā*. Buddhism emphasizes the importance of the scientific outlook in dealing with problems of morality and religion. Its specific 'dogmas are capable of verification.'[7] Its general account of the nature of man and the universe is one that accords with the findings of science.

Buddhist conception of the cosmos is similar to the modern conception of the universe. On more than one occasion, the Buddha has admonished honest seekers after the truth in the following words (Kālāma Sutta):

> Do not believe in what you have heard; do not believe in the traditions because they have been handed down

> for generations; do not believe in anything because it is rumoured and spoken by many; do not believe merely because a written statement of some old sage is produced; do not believe in conjectures, do not believe in that truth to which you have become attached by habit; do not believe merely the authority of your teachers and elders. After observation and analysis, when it agrees with reason and is conducive to the good and gain of one and all, then accept it and live up to it. Pray do not, therefore, believe me when I come to the philosophical issues until and unless you are convinced of what I say, either as a sequel to proper reasoning or by means of a practical approach.[8]

Kālāma Sutta is also called as first declaration of independent and rational thinking.

In Buddha's teachings, critical investigation and personal verification is the guide to true morality and religion. The Buddha said:

> If any one were to speak ill of me; my doctrine and my order, do not bear any ill-will towards him, be upset or perturbed at heart, for if you were to be so, it will only cause you harm. If on the other hand, any one were to speak well of me, my doctrine and my order, do not be overjoyed, thrilled or elated at heart, for if so it will only be an obstacle in your way of forming a correct judgement as to whether the quality is praised in us are real and actually found in us.[9]

As per Buddhist teachings, there are three laws, which govern the life and destiny of the individual. They are the Law of Continuity, which makes for the persistence of individuality (*Bhava*), the Law of Moral Retribution (*Kamma*) whereby morally good acts tend to result in pleasant consequences and morally evil acts in unpleasant consequences for the individual, and finally, the Law of Causal Genesis (*Paṭiccasamuppāda*) which is intended to explain the above two laws. Personal and direct knowledge of the operations of these three laws constitutes the three-fold knowledge (*Tisso Vijjā*), which the Buddha and his disciples claimed to have. Awareness of the fact and the way in which one is being conditioned results in one's ceasing to be conditioned, a state which corresponds to the attainment of the unconditioned and supreme felicity of *Nibbāna.* This is salvation in Buddhism, which is literally, salvation from the bondage of finite and conditioned existence. But actually, *Nibbāna* is beyond description or conception of the sensory organs because it is a state so radically different from the type of existent things we can conceive of. The Buddha preached that every person has got the seeds of *Nibbāna* within oneself. However, *Nibbāna* should be experienced by every person by walking on the path of *Dhamma.*

Dhamma is neither a Doctrine nor a Philosophy

Preaching to Dīghanakha (Sañjaya), the Buddha explained that "his teachings are neither a doctrine nor a philosophy".[10] It is not the result of discussion, debate or mental conjuctures and surmises like different philosophies which believe that the fundamental essence of the universe is fire, water, earth, wind or spirit, or that the universe is either finite or infinite, temporary or eternal. He explained that such assumptions about truth are like ants crawling round the rim of a bowl, reaching nowhere. His teachings are the result of his own direct experience. He preached that all things are impermanent, without a separate self, which he learned from his own direct experience. Anybody can experience it. Anybody can realize the Law of Dependent Origination. All things depend on all other things to arise, develop and pass away. Nothing is created from a single, original source. His goal was not to explain the universe but to help and guide others to have a direct experience of the real nature of things. Words cannot describe the truth. Only direct experience enables people to see the real nature of things and people can realize the truth only by direct experience.

The *Dhamma* expounds no dogmas that one must blindly believe, no creeds that one must accept on good faith without reasoning, no superstitious rites and ceremonies to be observed for formal entry into the fold, no meaningless sacrifices and penances for one's purification.

The Buddha exhorted his disciples to seek the truth, and not to heed mere persuasion even by a superior authority. Buddhists do not worship an image expecting worldly or spiritual favours, but pay their homage to what it represents. "A Buddhist goes before an image and offers flowers and incense not to the image but to the Buddha. He does so as a mark of gratitude, reflecting on the virtues of the Buddha and pondering on the transience of flowers. An understanding Buddhist designedly makes himself feel that he is in the noble presence of the Buddha, and thereby gains inspiration to emulate him." [11] Buddhists also do not worship the Bodhi-tree, but consider it a symbol of enlightenment, and so, worthy of reverence. These external objects of homage are not absolutely necessary, but they are useful and they help one to concentrate one's attention. An intellectual could dispense with them as he could easily focus his attention on the Buddha, and thus visualize him. **For our own good, and out of gratitude, we pay such homage, but what the Buddha expects from his disciples is not obeisance but the actual observance of his teaching.**

In the Buddha's teachings, there is no almighty god to be obeyed and feared. The existence of a supernatural power, conceived as the almighty being or a causeless force is of no importance in his teachings. There is neither divine revelation nor divine messengers or prophets. A Buddhist is, therefore, not subservient to any higher supernatural power which controls his destinies and which arbitrarily rewards and punishes. Since the Buddhists do not believe in revelations of a divine being, they do not claim the monopoly of truth and do not condemn any other religion. Intolerance is the greatest enemy of religion. With his characteristic tolerance, the Buddha advised his disciples not to get angry, discontented, or displeased even when others spoke ill of him or of his teaching or of his order. The Buddha said, "If you do so, you will not only bring yourselves into danger of spiritual loss, but you will also not be able to judge whether what they say is correct or not correct" - a very enlightened sentiment. Denouncing the criticism of other faiths the Buddha stated, "It is as a man who looks up and spits at heaven - the spittle does not soil heaven, but it comes back and defiles his own person." In the present time when incidents of communal violence are on the rise, the above preaching of the Buddha have become more relevant.

The Four Noble Truths and the Eightfold Noble Path, which lead to cessation of suffering are described below:

Four Noble Truths

1. Truth of Suffering (There is Suffering.)
2. Truth of Origin of Suffering (Suffering has causes: craving and aversion.)
3. Truth of Extinction of Suffering.
4. Truth of the Path Leading to the Extinction of Suffering.

Truth of Suffering

Suffering begins with the beginning of life. We have no conscious recollection of existence within the confines of the womb, but the common experience is that we emerge from it crying. Birth is a great trauma. There is suffering due to sickness and old age. No body wants to fall sick. No body wants to attain old age. But it is a fact of life that every body suffers due to some disease and everyone has to grow old. We become involved with the unpleasant and separated from the pleasant. We fail to get what we want, instead we get what we do not want. All these situations are suffering. No matter how sick we may be, no matter how old we may be, none of us wants to die. Thus, death is also suffering.

Truth of Origin of Suffering

The main cause of suffering is attachment to the five aggregates of mind and body. The Buddha said *saṅkhittena pañcupādāna-kkhandhā dukkhā* (in short, attachment to the five aggregates is suffering). One aggregate is the aggregate of body. The other four aggregates are of mind, namely perception, cognition, sensation and reaction. It is the result of inordinate attachment that each one of us has developed towards this body and mind. People cling strongly to their identity, their mental and physical being, when actually these are only evolving processes. This clinging to an unreal idea of oneself, to something that in fact is constantly changing, is a cause of suffering.

There are several types of attachment; first, there is attachment to the habit of seeking sensual pleasures because it gives rise to pleasant sensations. As soon as one desire is satisfied we generate another and we become habitual in craving. Our cravings become stronger and stronger as we fulfill them and so long as we crave we can never be happy, because there is no end to craving. Another attachment is to the 'I', the ego, the image we have of ourselves. We extend I to mine: whatever belongs to us and further to our views and our beliefs. Finally, there is attachment to religious forms and ceremonies. People tend to emphasize the external expressions of religion more than their underlying meaning and to feel that anyone who does not perform such ceremonies can not be a truly religious person. All our sufferings, whatever they may be, are connected to one or the other of these attachments. Attachments and sufferings are always found together. Practice of the Buddha's teaching eradicates this basic cause of misery.

Truth of Extinction of Suffering

By applying the Law of Dependent Origination, of cause and effect: if this exists, that occurs; that arises from the arising of this. If this does not exist that doesn't occur; that ceases from the ceasing of this. That means nothing happens without a cause. If the cause is eradicated there will be no effect. In this way, the process of the arising of the suffering can be reversed. If we put an end to ignorance, then there will be no blind reactions that bring in their wake all kinds of suffering. And if there is no more suffering, then we shall experience real peace, real happiness. The wheel of suffering can change into the wheel of liberation. We are ourselves responsible for the reactions that cause our suffering. By accepting our responsibility we can learn how to eliminate suffering.

The Buddha said: "By yourself committing wrong you defile yourself. By yourself not doing wrong, you purify yourself." [12]

There is a Path Leading to the Cessation of Suffering

The suffering can be eradicated by eradicating its causes: ignorance, craving and aversion. To achieve this goal the Budddha discovered, followed and taught a practical way to this attainable end. He called this way the *Ārya Ashatāṅgika Mārga,* that is, the Eight Fold Noble Path. He explained it in simple words,

> *Sabba-pāpassa akaraṇaṁ, Kusalassa upasampadā,*
> *Sa-citta-pariyodapanaṁ, Etaṁ Buddhāna Sāsanaṁ.* [13]

> (Abstain from all unwholesome deeds, perform wholesome ones, Purify your mind – this is the teaching

of the enlightened persons)

The Noble Eightfold Path is divided into three divisions of *Silā* (morality), *Samādhi* (mastery over mind) and *Paññā* (total purification of mind by wisdom and insight).

Silā is moral practice, abstention from all unwholesome actions of body and speech. Anyone who wishes to practice *Dhamma* must begin by practicing *Sīlā*, without this one cannot advance. We must abstain from all actions, all words and deeds, that harm other people. This is easily understood; society requires such behaviour in order to avoid disruption. But in fact we need to abstain from such actions because they harm ourselves. It is impossible to commit an unwholesome action - to insult, kill, steal or lie, or commit adultery - without generating great agitation in the mind, great craving and aversion. This moment of craving or aversion brings unhappiness now, and more in the future. The Buddha said:

Burning now, burning hereafter, the wrong-
doer suffers doubly
Happy now, happy hereafter, the virtuous
person doubly rejoices." [14]

Samādhi is the practice of concentration, developing the ability to consciously direct and control one's own mental processes. By practicing *sīlā* we attempt to control our speech and physical actions. However the cause of suffering lies in our mental actions. Merely restraining our words and deeds is useless if the mind continues to boil in craving and aversion, in unwholesome mental actions. Sooner or later the craving and aversion will erupt and we shall break *Silā*, harming others and ourselves. Thus mastery over mind is necessary. As the problem originates in the mind, we must confront it at the mental level. It can be achieved by *Samādhi*. The Buddha's sole objective of developing *Samādhi* was to have the purity and strength of mind essential for the realization of truth. We have in Buddhism forty different methods of concentration of which the most outstanding is *Ānāpāna Sati* i.e. concentration on the incoming and outgoing breath, the method followed by all the Buddhas.

Paññā is experiential wisdom, the development of purifying

insight into one's own nature. Right understanding of truth is the aim and object of *Dhamma*. Right aspiration is the analytical study of mind and matter, both within and without, in order to come to the realization of the truth. The Buddha repeatedly said:

> If it is supported by morality,
> concentration is very fruitful, very
> beneficial.
>
> If it is supported by concentration, wisdom
> is very fruitful, very beneficial.
>
> If it is supported by wisdom, the mind
> becomes free of all defilements.[15]

The path is an ascending spiral leading to liberation. Each of the three trainings supports the others, like the three legs of a tripod. The legs must all be present and of equal length or the tripod cannot stand.[16] The Buddha said:

> From right understanding proceeds right thought;
>
> from right thought proceeds right speech;
>
> from right speech proceeds right action;
>
> from right action proceeds right livelihood;
>
> from right livelihood proceeds right effort;
>
> from right effort proceeds right awareness;
>
> from right awareness proceeds right concentration;
>
> from right concentration proceeds right wisdom;
>
> from right wisdom proceeds right liberation. [17]

Morality *(sīlā)* and concentration *(samādhi)* are valuable, but their real purpose is to lead to wisdom. It is only by developing experiential wisdom *(paññā)* that one can penetrate into the reality within and free oneself of all ignorance and attachments. Some people may ask as to why precept has been kept first and not *Sammā Diṭṭhi* first as the Buddha did in the *Dhammacakkappavattana Sutta*. It needs to be explained that the Buddha was addressing the five ascetics who had already been practicing precepts and concentration for many years. For lay followers beginning has to be made from precepts. It is only after observing *Sīlā* that one can enter into *Samādhi* and then to *Paññā*. Moreover, *Sīlā*, *Samādhi* and *Paññā* are also like three pillars of a tripod. It can not stand in balance unless all three are strong. *Sīlā, Samādhi* and *Paññā* help each other and get strengthened from each other.

Eightfold Noble Path *(Ārya Ashatāṅgika Mārga)*

Paññā (Experiential Wisdom)

1. Right Understanding (*Sammā-Diṭṭhi*)

It is right understanding that is real wisdom. Thinking about truth is not enough, we must realize truth ourselves, and we must see things as they really are, not just as they appear to be. Apparent truth is a reality but that one must penetrate in order to experience the ultimate reality of ourselves and eliminate suffering.

Each one of us must live truth by direct experience, by the practice of *Vipassanā Bhāvanā* - only this living experience will liberate the mind. No one else's realization of truth will liberate us. Even the Enlightment of the Buddha could liberate only one person, Siddhāttha Gotama. At most, someone else's realization can act as an inspiration for others, offering guidelines for them to follow, but ultimately we must do the work ourselves. As the Buddha said:

> *'Tumehi kiccaṁ atappaṁ akkhātāro tathāgatā'*[18]
>
> (You have to do your own work; those who have reached the goal will only show the way.)

Truth can be lived, can be experienced directly, only within oneself; whatever is outside is always at a distance from us. Only within can we have actual, direct, living experience of reality.

2. Right Thought (*Sammā-Saṅkappo*)

The Right Thought free from greed and sensuous desire, aiming at an escape from the cycle of rebirth; thought for the welfare of all living beings and for the non-injury of all living beings.

Sīlā (*Morality*)

3. Right Speech (*Sammā-Vācā*)

By right speech is meant speech which must be true, beneficial and neither foul nor malicious.

4. Right Action *(Sammā-Kammanto)*

By right action is meant fundamental morality, which is opposed to killing, stealing, sexual misconduct and consumption of intoxicants.

5. Right Livelihood *(Sammā-Ājīvo)*

Right livelihood means ways of living by trade/occupation/ profession other than those, which increase the suffering of all beings, such as slave trade, flesh trade, immoral trafficking, manufacturing and trading of weapons, gambling, and trafficking in intoxicating drugs/substances, taking bribes/illegal gratification, fooling others by conducting rites and rituals in the name of god and heaven, spreading superstitions.

Samādhi (*Mastery over Mind*)

6. Right Effort (*Sammā-Vāyāmo*)

Right effort is the prerequisite for right awareness. Unless one makes a concerted effort to narrow down the range of thoughts of his wavering and unsteady mind, he cannot expect to secure that awareness of mind which in turn helps him bring the mind by right concentration to a state of focus and equanimity.

The most suitable technique for exploring inner reality is *Ānāpāna-Sati*, awareness of respiration. Respiration is an object of attention that is readily available to everyone, because we all breathe from the time of birth untill the time of death. It is a universally accessible, universally acceptable object of meditation. The Buddha described the four types of right effort:

i. To prevent evil, unwholesome states from arising;
ii. To abandon them if they should arise;
iii. To generate wholesome states not yet existing; and
iv. To maintain them without lapse, causing them to develop and to reach full growth and perfection.

By practicing awareness of respiration, we practice all four right efforts.

7. Right Awareness (*Sammā-Sati*)

Right awareness means knowledge about true happening in the body from moment to moment. Observing respiration results in right awareness. Suffering arises due to ignorance. People react because they do not know what they are doing, because of lack of knowledge about happenings in the body. 'The mind spends most of its time lost in fantasies, illusions, reliving pleasant and unpleasant experiences and anticipating the future with eagerness or fear.'[19] The present moment is the only moment. Nobody can live in the past; it is gone. Nor can anybody live in the future; as the future never comes. It will come only as present moment. Therefore, we can live only in the present. If we are not aware of our present moments, we are bound to repeat the mistakes of the past again and again. As a result, we can not succeed in attaining our future goals. But if we can develop the habit of being alert about the present moment, we can use the past for guiding our present actions. *Dhamma* is the path of here-and-now. It helps us in developing the ability to be aware of the present moment. We need a method to concentrate the attention on the reality of the moment. The practice of *Ānāpāna-Sati* helps us in developing the ability to be aware of the present moment. By regular practice of awareness of respiration, we become aware of the present moment.

The awareness of breathing helps us in removing negativity of the mind and achieving the goal of complete liberation.

8. Right Concentration (*Sammā-Samādhi*)

The right concentration is meant to maintain the awareness from moment to moment, for as long as possible. Samādhi must have as its focus an object that is free from all craving, all aversion, all illusions.

Importance of Mind

The Buddha gave prime importance to mind. Any action is preceded by thought in mind. Whether our actions are good or bad depends upon the quality of our thoughts. The progress of mankind depends on the quality of mental thoughts.

The Buddha said one would become what one thinks to become. Therefore, one should think that what one would like to become. Among all the resources of development, the greatest is the "will to improve". Millions and millions of people all over the world do not have any will to improve because they have been told that their present conditions/problems are due to the sins committed by them in their earlier births or due to the original sins committed by their forefathers. The Buddha said that one is the master of one's destiny. If one has a will to improve, no power in the universe can stop him/her from progressing. But if one's conduct and actions are bad, no power in the universe can save him/her from suffering. The Buddha is like a good physician who diagnoses the cause of suffering and then by prescribing treatment in the form of *Vipassanā* meditation, he cures the disease of suffering.

Describing the primacy of mind, the Buddha said:

Mano-pubbaṅgamā dhammā, mano-seṭṭhā, mano-mayā.

Manasā ce paduṭṭhena bhāsati vā karoti vā,

Tato naṁ dukkhamanveti cakkaṁ' va vahato padaṁ.

Mano-pubbaṅgamā dhammā, mano-seṭṭhā, mano-mayā.

Manasā ce pasannena bhāsati vā karoti vā,

tato nam sukkhamanveti Chāyā 'va anapāyinī [20]

(Mind precedes all phenomena, mind matters most, every thing is mind-made

If with an impure mind one performs any action of speech or body, then suffering will follow that person as the cartwheel follows the foot of the draught animal

Mind precedes all phenomena, mind matters most, every thing is mind-made.

If with a pure mind one performs any action of speech or body, then happiness will follow that person as a shadow that never departs.)

The teachings of the Buddha are a practical solution to all our problems. Unlike other teachers, the Buddha never used the tools of allurement and fear in future births. His teachings are for here and now. Therefore, we ourselves can see the result of our good or bad actions. His teachings that enmity cannot be overcome by enmity, the fire can not be extinguished by fire, the war can not be a solution to our problems, are worth following.

Thus, practice of morality (*sīlā*), mastery over mind (*samādhi*), experiential wisdom (*paññā*), loving kindness (*mettā bhāvanā*) towards all beings, equality and fraternity among fellow citizens and continuous striving for the welfare of all beings is the essence of *Dhamma*. By practising *sīlā, samādhi and paññā* we can liberate ourselves from the miseries of life caused due to craving and aversion.

The Buddha emphasized on the practical aspects of *Dhamma* instead of mere theoretical knowledge. He explained how we ourselves are responsible for making our life miserable. We distribute this misery to others also, as we can distribute only what we have. He explained that it won't help if somebody only recites the *suttas* of his preaching without practicing them in his daily life. Such persons are like herdmen who take others' cattle for grazing and return them to the owner after carefully accounting without getting a drop of milk from such cows. Similarly, if somebody only recites the *suttas* without practicing them, he will not get even a drop of *Dhamma* nectar.

The *Dhamma* makes one stand on his own feet and rouses self-confidence and energy only when one walks on the path of *Dhamma*. It aims to produce in every man a thorough internal transforming by self-conquest. The Buddha has only shown the way to salvation, and it is left to each individual to decide for himself if he would follow it.

The Buddha found that there is always a cause, which results in an event. He described this cause-action relationship as *Paṭiccasamuppāda* (the Law of Dependent Origination). Without understanding *paṭiccasamuppāda,* it is difficult to change conditioned reactions of mind and break the unending chain of birth and death. Therefore, the working of the Law of Dependent Origination is explained in the next chapter.

"Transient are all conditioned things, Sorrowful are all conditioned things,
Soulless are all conditioned and non-conditioned
DHAMMAPADA

Chapter 4

The Law of Dependent Origination (Paṭiccasamuppāda)

The Law of Dependent Origination *(Paṭiccasamuppāda)* is the unique discovery of the Buddha. Nothing happens without a cause. As every event, big or small, has a cause behind it, so has every cause an effect. This cause-effect relationship is the foundation of the Buddha's teachings. The law applies to every entity, living or dead, big or small, from micro-level to macro-level, from individual to communities, from societies to nations.

We can see the working of this law all round us. If there is terrorism and violence in the world, it means people have hatred and fear in their hearts and minds and they perceive that governments are not mitigating their grievances. If there is corruption, it means people are greedy and not living a moral life. If somebody is poor; its cause may be either he is not working or he is spending more than what he is earning or somebody is exploiting him and enjoying the fruits of his labour. Similarly, if we are sick, it means we must have caught infection or we are not getting enough food or we are over-eating or we are not exercising enough or we are leading an undisciplined life. There can be a number of reasons. But the fundamental fact is that there is always a reason behind every act we do or every difficulty we face or everything happening around us.

Therefore, *Paṭiccasamuppāda* can also be called the law of cause-effect relationship. No entity in the universe is independent in absolute terms. Everything depends for its existence on other things. A tree needs soil, water, air and sunlight for its survival. Stars and planets need gravitational force to remain in their orbits. A man needs food, water and oxygen for his survival. Business and industry need peace, law and order, infrastructure, manpower, capital, and markets for their growth. Everything is dependent on other things. Therefore, *Paṭiccasamuppāda* is also called the Law of Dependent Origination. The Buddha said:

> Yo Paṭiccasamuppādaṁ passati, so dhammaṁ passati.
> Yo dhammam passati, so Paṭiccasamuppādaṁ passati.
> One who sees *Paṭiccasamuppāda* sees the *Dhamma*.
> One who sees the *Dhamma* sees *Paṭiccasamuppāda*.[1]

Paṭicca means 'because of' or 'dependent upon' and *Samuppāda* means 'arising' or 'originating from'. Although the literal meaning of the term is arising because of or dependent arising or origination, it is applied to the whole causal formula that consists of twelve inter-dependent causes and effects, which are technically called *Paccaya* and *Paccayuppannā*.

The Buddha said:

> *Imasmiṁ sati, idaṁ hoti, imasmiṁ asati, idaṁ na hoti.*[2]
> (If this is, that comes to be; from the arising of this, that arises; if this is not, that doesn't come to be; from the stopping of this, that is stopped.)

Paṭiccasamuppāda is a discourse on the process of birth and death. It deals with the cause of rebirth and suffering with a view to helping men get rid of the ills of life. Ignorance (*Avijjā*) of the truth of suffering, its cause, its end, and the way to its end, is the chief cause that sets the wheel of life in motion. It is the lack of knowledge of things as they truly are, or of oneself as one really is. It clouds all right understanding. When ignorance is destroyed and turned into knowledge, all causality is shattered as in the case of the Buddhas and *Arahatas.* One becomes *Arahata* when all the defilements of mind are removed. The mind becomes pure and no trace of any defilement is left. One becomes free from the chain of birth and death. No re-birth is possible. Similarly, one becomes a Buddha when he perfects all ten *Pāramitās* and breaks the chain of birth and death and goes beyond the cycle of *samsāra*. Every Buddha is an *Arahata* but every *Arahata* is not a Buddha. Ignorance of the past, future, or both past and future, and the dependent origination is also considered as *Avijjā.*

The Buddha said:

Anuloma (*Forward Order*)

Avijjā-paccayā saṇkhāra; saṇkhāra-paccayā viññānaṁ; Viññāna-paccayā nāma-rūpaṁ; nāma-rūpa-paccayā salāyatanaṁ; Salāyatana-paccayā phasso; phassa-paccayā vedana; Vedanā-paccayā taṇhā; taṇhā-paccayā upādānaṁ; Upādānaṁ-paccayā bhavo; bhava-paccayā jāti; Jāti-paccayā-jarā-maraṇam-soka-parideva-dukkha- domanassupāyāsa sambhavanti. Evametassa kevalassa dukkhakkhandhassa samudayo hoti. [3]

Which means:
With the base of ignorance, reaction arises;
With the base of reaction, consciousness arises;
With the base of consciousness, mind and body arise;
With the base of mind and body, the six senses arise;
With the base of the six senses, contact arises;
With the base of contact, sensation arises;
With the base of sensation, craving and aversion arise;
With the base of craving and aversion, attachment arises;
With the base of attachment, the process of becoming arises;
With the base of the process of becoming, birth arises;
With the base of birth, ageing and death arise, together with sorrow, lamentation, physical and mental sufferings and tribulations.
Thus arises this entire mass of suffering.

Patiloma (*Reverse Order*):

Avijjāya eva asesa-viraga-nirodhā, saṇkhāra-nirodho saṇkhāra-nirodhā viññāna-nirodho, viññāna-nirodhā nama-rūpa-nirodho;
Nama-rūpa-nirodhā salāyatana-nirodho; salāyatana-nirodhā phassa-nirodho;
Phassa-nirodhā vedana-nirodho; vedana nirodhā tanha-

nirodho
tanha nirodhā upādāna-nirodho, upādāna-nirodhā bhava-nirodho;
Bhava-nirodhā jati-nirodho;
Jati-nirodhā jarā-maranam-soka-parideva-dukkha-domanssupayasa nirujjhanti.
Evametassa kevalassa dukkhakkhandassa nirodho hoti.[4]

Which means:

With the complete eradication and cessation of ignorance, reaction ceases;
With the cessation of reaction, consciousness ceases;
With the cessation of consciousness, mind and body cease;
With the cessation of mind and body, the six senses cease;
With the cessation of the six senses, contact ceases;
With the cessation of contact, sensation ceases;
With the cessation of sensation, craving and aversion cease;
With the cessation of craving and aversion, attachment ceases;
With the cessation of attachment, the process of becoming ceases;
With the cessation of the process of becoming, birth ceases;

With the cessation of birth, ageing and death cease, together with sorrow, lamentation, physical and mental sufferings and tribulations;

Thus this entire mass of suffering ceases.

The Buddha discovered that between the object and the reactions there is a missing link: *Vedanā* (sensation). We react not to exterior reality but to the sensations within us. *Vedanā* has both mental and physical aspects. Matter alone cannot feel anything if the mind is not present. A dead body, for example, has no sensation. It is the mind that feels, but what it feels has an inextricable physical element. This physical element is of central importance in practicing the teachings of the Buddha. The purpose of this practice is to develop in us the ability to deal with all the vicissitudes of life in a balanced way. We learn to do so in *Vipassanā* meditation by observing with equanimity whatever happens within ourselves. With this equanimity, we can break the habit pattern of blind reaction, and instead can choose the most beneficial course of action in any situation.

Whatever we experience in life is encountered through the six gates of perception, the five physical senses and the mind. According to the Law of Dependent Origination, as soon as a contact occurs at any of these six gates, as soon as we encounter any phenomenon, physical or mental, a sensation is produced. If we do not give attention to what happens in the body, we remain unaware; unconscious reaction begins toward the sensation, a momentary liking or disliking, which develops into craving or aversion.

The habit pattern of mind is such that like a pendulum, it does not want to remain stable and in peace. It always wants to remain linked either with craving or with aversion.

Whenever any of the six sensory organs (eyes, nose, tongue, ears, skin and mind) come in contact with their objects (seeing, smelling, tasting, hearing, touching and thoughts, respectively), we 'cognise' them and then our 'perception' evaluates the object on the basis of the stored information and passes a value judgment. Based on this value judgment, be it pleasant or unpleasant, sensations arise in the body. If a sensation is pleasant, we want to have more of it and generate a craving for it; if a sensation is unpleasant, then we do not want to have it and develop an aversion for it. In this way, we generate three kinds of *Saṅkhāra-s* or reactions.

The first kind of *saṇkhāra*-s is like a line drawn in the water. We read newspapers, watch television, see whatsapp, messages or listen to the radio daily. When we come across any pleasant news, we feel happy. But when news is unpleasant, we feel sad. This is because we react to news as per our likes and dislikes and beliefs. These reactions create impressions in our mind. Majority of these daily impressions get evaporated from the mind like a line drawn in the water. If we are asked to explain what we read in a newspaper on a particular day or what we ate the previous month, we won't be able to tell even though we might have reacted to the news of that day and might have enjoyed food on that day, because the *saṇkhāra*-s are so transient, and cannot be recollected easily.

The second kind of *saṇkhāra*-s or imprints represent a bit

more permanency, say something like a line drawn on the beach sand, the life of which is dependent on the modality of the tidal rising. These imprints created on the mind take some time in getting evaporated. Some important events like passing/failure in an important examination, festivals, birthdays, anniversaries etc fall into this category. These imprints can be recollected with a little effort.

Third kind of *saṇkhāra*-s is like the line drawn on a rock that is long lasting. Some very important events which have created very strong emotions and reactions in our life such as first love or first job, marriage, death/parting of near and dear ones, public insult, disease, etc. These imprints create strong emotions/ reactions in our mind automatically and keep on multiplying. Very little effort is required to recollect these imprints. Irrespective of whether they are pleasant or unpleasant, they make us restless.

This reaction is repeated and intensified innumerable times before it impinges on the conscious mind. If the practitioners of *Vipassanā* meditation give importance only to what happens in the conscious mind, they become aware of the process after the reaction has occurred and gathered dangerous proportions sufficient to overwhelm them. They allow the spark of sensation to ignite a raging fire before trying to extinguish it, needlessly creating difficulties for themselves. But if they learn to observe the sensations, within the body objectively, they permit each spark to burn itself out without starting a conflagration. By giving importance to the physical aspect, they become aware of the *Vedanā* as soon as it arises, and can prevent any adverse reactions from occurring.

The physical aspect of *Vedanā* is particularly important because it offers a vivid, tangible experience of the reality of impermanence within us. Change occurs at every moment within us, manifesting itself in the play of sensations. It is at this level that impermanence must be experienced. Observation of the constantly changing sensations leads to the realisation of one's own ephemeral nature. This realisation makes obvious the futility of attachment to something that is so transitory. Thus, the direct experience of *Anicca* automatically gives rise to detachment, with which one can not only aver fresh reactions of craving or aversion, but also eliminate the very habit of reacting. In this way one gradually frees the mind from suffering.

By observing sensations with equanimity, one can eliminate ignorance and penetrate the delusion of self-ego. When one experiences the impermanence, the ever-changing nature of sensations, realisation comes that there is nothing that can be called self, me or mine. Thus comes the realisation of *Anātmavāda* or non-existence of the self or soul. Unless its physical aspect is included, the awareness of *Vedanā* remains incomplete. It is because of this, the Buddha repeatedly emphasised the importance of the experience of impermanence through physical sensations. He said those who continually make efforts:

> *"To direct their awareness toward the body,*
> *Who abstain from unwholesome actions*
> *And strive to do what should be done,*
> *Such people, aware, with full understanding,*
> *Are freed from their defilements."*

The cause of suffering is *Taṇhā*, that is craving and aversion. Ordinarily, it appears to us that we generate reactions of craving and aversion toward various objects that we encounter through the physical senses and the mind. The Buddha, however, discovered that between the object and the reaction stands a missing link, that is *Vedanā*. We react not to the exterior reality but to the sensations within. Any addiction to intoxicating substances is not addicted to the substances per se but to the sensation that such substances produce in the body. When we learn to observe sensation without reacting to craving and aversion, the cause of suffering does not arise at all and suffering ceases. Therefore, observation of *Vedanā* is essential to practice what the Buddha taught. The observation must be at the level of physical sensation if the awareness of *Vedanā* is to be complete. With the awareness of physical sensations we can penetrate to the root of the problem and remove it. We can observe our own nature to the depths and can liberate ourselves from suffering.

By understanding the central importance of the observation of sensation in the teachings of the Buddha, one can gain fresh insights into the *Satipaṭṭhāna-sutta*. The above *Sutta* explains that practice of *Satipaṭṭhāna*, helps in establishing awareness: purification of beings; transcendence of sorrow and lamentation; extinguishing of physical and mental suffering; practicing of a way of truth and the direct experience of the ultimate reality, *Nibbāna*." By practicing *Satipaṭṭhāna* a meditator dwells ardently with thorough understanding and awareness, sensations, mind, – mental contents, observing the contents of the mind, having abandoned craving and aversion toward the world. He is aware of his mental and physical phenomena which are changing from moment to moment. The practitioner observes body in body, mind in mind, sensation in sensation and so forth.

For a *Vipassanā* practitioner, the experience is luminous when he or she realises that these are the four dimensions of a human being. To understand this human phenomenon correctly, each one of us must experience the reality of ourselves directly. To achieve this direct experience, the practitioner must develop two qualities: awareness (*Sati*) and thorough understanding (*Sampajañña*). The discourse is called "the establishing of awareness", but awareness is incomplete without understanding insights into the depths of one's own nature, into the impermanence of this phenomenon that one calls 'I'. The practice of *Satipaṭṭhāna* leads the practitioners to realise their essentially ephemeral nature. When they have had this personal realisation, then awareness is firmly established, right awareness leading to liberation. Then automatically craving and aversion disappear, not just towards the external world but also towards the world within, where cravings and aversions are most deep-seated, and most often overlooked — in the unthinking, visceral attachment to one's own body and mind. So long as this underlying attachment remains, one cannot be liberated from suffering. Lord Buddha discovered that if we can break the chain at the stage of 'sensation' (Vedanā) by remaining equidistant from both pleasant and unpleasant sensations and by observing the sensations as they are and not trying to change as we want them to be, we can reverse the cycle of suffering and entire mass of suffering ceases. With the cessation of suffering, one becomes free from illusion, fear, anger or desire. He gets filled with peace, joy, love and understanding. One overcomes forgetfulness and becomes mindful of every moment. With awareness one can attain total freedom, peace and joy.

We suffer due to fear, hatred, jealousy, attachment, greed, lust, desire etc. and because of false belief in the existence of 'ego' or 'self'. We treat impermanent as permanent, external as internal and vice versa. But with direct experience of impermanence one realises the non-existence of any sensation, or phenomenon or things independently or in isolation. Every phenomenon or event is dependent on so many other things. For example 'if we take a leaf of any tree and see it with awareness we can realise the presence of the sun, earth, water and wind in it because without the sunlight, water, earth and wind a leaf cannot exist.'[5] This applies to every entity in the world. Every event is a reflection of its causes. The seed is the indicator of the presence of the tree and vice versa. The Buddha said that instead of debating as to whether the seed came first or tree came first, one should concentrate on the impermanence of everything that would liberate the suffering people from the chain of birth and death.

However, it needs to be emphasized that one cannot fully appreciate the law of dependent origination by only reading the books or by hearing a discourse or by discussions; to understand it properly, one needs to actually experience it for which one has to learn *Vipassanā* meditation. While *Paṭiccasamuppāda* explains the theory, *Vipassanā* meditation is the practical side of this.

Chapter 5
Vipassanā Meditation

Vipassanā is one of the most ancient meditation techniques of India. It was discovered about 2,550 years ago by Gotama the Buddha. During His time, millions of people in India were freed from the bondages of sufferings by practicing *Vipassanā*, which also made them attain high levels of achievement in all spheres of life. Over a period of time, the technique spread to the neighbouring countries like Myanmar, Sri Lanka, Vietnam and Thailand, where it brought the same ennobling effect.

In multi-religious and multi-cultural societies *Vipassanā* is a wonderful and practical path to achieve unity in diversity. This ancient and timeless heritage of India is in a way the quintessence of all religions' teaching how to live a moral life, to purify one's mind and be its master. *Vipassanā* is an effective and universal method to gain these ideals.

This technique prevailed in the country for many centuries. Thereafter, this technique got polluted due to mixing of many things like imagination, verbalisation, and incorrect assumptions, due to which it did not yield the desired results. People stopped practicing this meditation. Gradually, *Vipassanā* found its way out of the country. Fortunately, in neighbouring Mynamar, the original form of *Vipassanā* was preserved in its pristine purity through the millennia, thanks to some devoted teachers.

The technique of *Vipassanā* was brought back to India from Myanmar in 1969 by the renowned industrialist Mr. S.N. Goenka, who dedicated his life for spreading the message of *Dhamma*. Acharya Goenka was authorised to teach *Vipassanā* by the renowned Burmese *Vipassanā* teacher Sayagyi U Ba Khin.

Mr. Sayagyi had the strong desire that *Vipassanā* should return to the land of its origin, India, so that the country could come out of its manifold problems. He was sure that from India it would then spread throughout the world for the benefit of all of mankind. Today, *Vipassanā* meditation is practiced by millions every day in more than 227 *Vipassanā* centres spread across the world. There are 107 regular centres in India and 120 abroad in addition to many makeshift facilities in various national academies, colleges, jails and other places.

The Meaning of Vipassanā

Vipassanā is a *Pāli* word, and it means 'insight'. To put it exactly, it means "seeing things as they really are." The term *Vipassanā* has two components, namely '*vi*' and '*passanā*'. '*Vi*' means 'minutely', 'perfectly', 'exactly', 'sincerely', 'inwardly', 'intrinsically' etc; '*passanā*' means 'looking', 'observing', 'analysing', 'introspecting', 'investigating' etc. Thus, literally it means observing things minutely, as they really are.

Vipassanā also means 'observing oneself in a special way'. It is a technique that purifies the mind, eradicating the negative effects of anger, hatred, greed, and selfishness through self- observation and introspection. In short it means 'insight meditation'. It is looking at things as they really are and not through coloured glasses. It is an effort to change the deep- rooted habit patterns of the mind, which dwell in the continuous blind reactions of craving and aversion.

Everything in the universe is vibrating. The only difference is in the degree of vibrations. To a casual observer, a piece of iron is motionless. The scientist, however, knows that it is composed of electrons, which are in a state of perpetual flux. Similarly, a lot of changes are taking place in the human body every moment due to electromagnetic and biochemical reactions. Mind and body are continuously interacting with each other, impacting each other and getting affected by each other. When the mind is thinking about something, say a pleasant thought, the body generates pleasant sensations. When thoughts are unpleasant, the body begins to generate unpleasant sensations. These sensations are continuously changing. When we have pleasant sensations moved by any reason, say our attraction to somebody, receiving a promotion, recognition, reward or award, flattery, or getting anything desirable, we yearn for more of them. In turn we develop a feeling of craving for such things and it further generates pleasant sensations. The same kind of chain actions take place when we watch a movie, read a book or dance. But, when we face criticism, condemnation, insults, humiliation, injury, loss, or anything that is not according to our expectations or desires, we generate unpleasant sensations, and then we start developing aversions to such unpleasant sensations. Over the years, we go on accumulating a stock of cravings and aversions, which make our lives more and more miserable. We lose sleep and develop insomnia, develop diseases and finally lose our peace of mind due to these cravings and aversions. And we do not restrict our miseries to ourselves. We distribute them to whoever comes in contact with us. As a result, we disturb the peace of our family, society, country and the universe, because we want to change everything around us as per our wishes and our desires.

We want to change others as per our beliefs. We want others to behave according to our desires. We want to reward those who conform to our norms and desires and punish those who do not. We say we would be happy if such and such thing happens, or we would have been happy if such and such would not have happened. We never say we are happy with the present circumstances. We always want either something to happen or something not to happen, as per our wishes. Due to this, there are continuous conflicts and turmoil in our families, societies, nations and the universe. But if we realise our true nature and see the impermanence of pleasant and unpleasant sensations, we will be able to make ourselves happy and bring about peace and harmony around us. The practice of *Vipassanā* meditation enables one to liberate oneself from the clutches of cravings and aversions, which leads to a happy, peaceful, harmonious, and liberated life.

Vipassanā, therefore, is a process of self-purification through self-observation and introspection. It is a technique of non- verbal, self-administered psycho-analysis that sets in motion the process of tension-release. One attains not only the ability to surgically operate on his mind, but also observe it just like a detached witness.

The following Pāli Sutta explains Vipassanā:
Vividhen passatī' ti Vipassanā, Visesena passatī' ti Vipassanā
Anekaṅgena passatī' ti Vipassanā
Vibhajjena passatī' ti Vipassanā.[1]

(We have to observe the reality by dividing it into small parts; we have to see the reality in a special way, we have to see the reality from different angles; and we have to see it with minute observations.)

Gotama the Buddha, the super-scientist of the physical- mental world, rediscovered certain universal truths, unknown to humanity until then. He discovered these fundamental truths without using any external instruments or laboratory equipment. He discovered these truths by directly experiencing these very truths, using his own body and mind as the laboratory instruments. He discovered that there is actually no solidity in the entire universe and that all material phenomena are made up of tiny *kalāpa-s* (sub-atomic particles). These *kalāpa-s* are not solid but arise and pass away with such great rapidity that they give the appearance of solidity. These *kalāpa-s*, which are the basic building blocks of the material universe, are nothing but mere vibrations.

The Buddha said:

Sabbo adīpito loko,
Sabbo loko padhupito;
Sabbo pajjalito loko,
Sabbo loko pakampito. [2]

The entire world is in flames,
The entire world is going up in smoke;
The entire world is burning,
The entire world is vibrating.

This discovery came to him through experiencing the different physical sensations arising and fading in the body, arising with pleasant, unpleasant or neutral feelings in the body. He also discovered that misery arises out of blind reaction to craving and aversion to these sensations. All this happens due to ignorance of how one is causing misery to oneself by reacting to these sensations.

The Buddha also discovered that the key to liberation lies in these very sensations. One comes out of the habit pattern of misery when one learns how to remain equanimous with every sensation, be it pleasant or unpleasant, with the experiential realisation that they are all impermanent, *Anicca* (the Pāli word for 'change' or 'impermanence'), changing every moment. This ability to remain equanimous to both these extremes eradicates old impurities and helps one change the behaviour pattern of the mind.

Misery arises because of defilements such as anger, hatred, jealousy, ill-will, passion, animosity, insecurity, depression, fear etc. Unless one learns to dispassionately observe these defilements along with the relative sensations, one is purifying only the surface of the mind and not the deeper layers, where our actual problems remain.

Vipassanā Teacher Sayagyi U Ba Khin
(March 6,1899-January 19,1971)

Vipassanā Teacher Shri S. N. Goenka
(Born in 1924-29th September, 2013)

Once one becomes established in this technique of observing the reality from within and with equanimity, it becomes very clear that human society cannot be categorized as high or low on basis of birth. A person understands that his or her high or low status depends on the purity or impurity of the mind. Then wrong understanding of caste, creed or religion based discrimination gets totally uprooted, and one can understand that it is the defiled or undefiled mind that determines one's actual social position, because this can determine whether one is serving or harming the society. One also realises that every person with a defiled mind can attain a higher position by purifying one's mind. With proper practice of *Vipassanā* meditation anyone can reach the highest level of total purification of the mind.

This is the process of purification that one undergoes during the *Vipassanā* retreat, the same path of discovery that the Buddha walked on to attain full Enlightenment. At the beginning of the *Vipassanā* retreat, the student undertakes a vow of moral behaviour. The student experiences how morality is the essential foundation of inner peace and happiness, and it is not merely an empty, unrealistic ideal. One cannot do any harm to others without first harming oneself:

Pubbe hanati ataman, pacchā hanati so pare.[3]

This is the experiential truth that inmates in many prisons worldwide realise after taking *Vipassanā* courses, which help them come out of the cycle of harming themselves by harming others. They experience the suffering of the gross, unpleasant sensations within, the hell-fires of burning, combustion and agitation at the level of sensations that someone usually experiences whenever a strong defilement arises in the mind. The fact is that the supreme experience was there always, but they were ignorant of this reality within. *Vipassanā* helps one break this barrier of ignorance and realise that one has to live a wholesome life, not merely to please others, but to first ensure peace and harmony for oneself. They realise that thoughts, words and actions of anger and violence turn them first into victims, before they harm their victims. This is the truth everyone experiences, inside and outside prisons.

How to Practise Vipassanā?

Vipassanā retreats are conducted at recognised *Vipassanā* centres free of charge.To learn *Vipassanā*, it is necessary to undertake a ten-day residential retreats under the guidance of a qualified teacher/guide. The retreats are conducted at established *Vipassanā* centres and other sites all over the world. During the retreat, students remain within the meditation centres, completely detached from the world outside. They have to even refrain from reading and writing, and suspend any religious practices or other disciplines. They also observe complete silence; however, they are free to discuss meditation questions with the teacher and material problems with the management. This helps them concentrate and focus their energy solely on the meditaton.

There are three steps in the practice: first, the students practise abstinence from actions that cause harm. They undertake five moral precepts, practicing abstention from killing, stealing, lying, sexual misconduct and the use of intoxicants. Observing these precepts calms down the mind, and helps it remain concentrated, focused and sharp.

Abstention from Killing: No living being wants to be killed or hurt. None of us, irrespective of our age, health or status, likes to be killed or hurt. Just as we don't wish that anybody should hurt or kill us, in the same way, no living being wishes to be hurt or killed. What is true for us is true for others as well.

The Buddha concludes: "A person who loves the self should not harm the self of others". Therefore, to maintain peace and law and order in society, we should not do anything to others that we would not like to be done for ourselves. This is the simple, apparent reality. But when one starts meditating and observing his breath, he would realise that no person can kill any living being unless one generates anger in the mind. No one can kill with a smile or happiness. We cannot even shout at any person unless we have generated anger. The moment anger is generated in us the respiration loses its normal rhythm; it becomes very fast and deep. Our normal heartbeat also changes, because of the electromagnetic and biochemical reactions taking place between our mind and body. Whenever anger is generated, a lot of harmful chemical substances are also generated. Therefore, before harming others, we are harming ourselves by generating anger. It is, therefore, necessary that we should abstain from killing.

Abstention from Stealing: No person wishes any of his/ her belongings to be stolen. Irrespective of the value of an article, none of us wish that somebody should steal our belongings. Just as we do not wish to have our belongings stolen, so it is with everybody else. This is the apparent reality for practicing abstention from stealing. But at a subtler level, when someone starts meditating and observing his breath, he realises that no person can steal anything, unless he generates greed in his mind. The moment greed arises, respiration loses its normal rhythm and becomes very fast and deep. Whenever greed is generated, a lot of harmful chemical substances are also generated. Therefore, before harming others, we are harming ourselves by generating greed. It is therefore, necessary that we abstain from stealing.

Abstention from Sexual Misconduct: No person wishes that someone commit adultery on any of his relatives or family members, be it a father or mother, son or daughter or brother or sister. If a relative is found to be indulging in sexual misconduct, one feels unhappy. Just as we do not like this to happen to our family and relatives, others also don't like this to happen to their family members and relatives. But at a subtler level, one can realise through *Vipassanā* meditation that no one can commit sexual misconduct unless one generates lust in the mind. The moment lust arises the respiration loses its normal rhythm and a lot of harmful chemical substances are also generated. Therefore, before harming another person, we are harming ourselves by generating lust. It is, therefore, necessary to abstain from sexual misconduct.

Abstention from Lying: No one likes to be lied to or get backbitten. Whenever one comes to know that a colleague or friend has lied/complained against him, one feels sad. Just as one does not like someone lying against him or somebody backbiting him, others also dislike it. What one does not like to happen to oneself, others also do not like to happen to them. But at a subtler level, one who practices *Vipassanā* meditation can realise that no person can lie or backbite, unless one generates envy, fear, hatred, greed etc. in one's own mind. The moment envy arises, respiration loses its normal rhythm and a lot of harmful chemical substances are generated. Therefore, before harming other persons, we are harming ourselves by generating envy. Therefore, it is necessary to abstain from lying.

Abstention from Using Intoxicants: Whenever intoxicants are used, the heart beat changes. The person under the influence of intoxicants loses control over his mind. As a result, he may forget to observe the above precepts and may harm himself as well as others. Intoxicants create a particular type of sensation in the user's body and the user develops a craving for such sensations. Intoxicants also kill many cells of the mind and reduce the sensitivity of the mind, making it impossible to observe sensations minutely. It is, therefore, essential to keep off intoxicants.

Western scientists have found that our mind is the cause of 80 percent of our ailments. The main cause for illnesses such as rashes, diabetes, backache and heart attack is defilements of our mind through anger, jealousy, hatred, tension and stress. Psychiatrists have found that though there is temporary relief for these illnesses through medication, illnesses recur because their causes remain within our minds.

The studies on scanning at the Wisconsin University at Madison, US, show activity in the left prefrontal lobes of meditation practitioners. The area is linked to positive emotions, self-control and temperament.

Other research by Paul Ekman of the University of California, San Francisco Medical Centre suggests that meditation and mindfulness can tame the amygdala, an area of the brain that is the hub of fear memory.

Ekman has discovered that practitioners of meditation are less likely to be shocked, flustered, surprised or as angry as the non-practitioners of meditation.

Flanagan writes in a report in the *New Scientist* magazine, "The most reasonable hypothesis is that there is something about conscientious Buddhist practice that results in the kind of happiness we all seek."

How does it Affect Health?

Whenever anger, hatred, jealousy, greed and lust is generated in us, discomforts are first felt at the cerebral cortex, the outer section of the brain. About 13 billion nerve cells get activated in receiving these feelings and about 10 billion of them are within the brain. Messages run across the nerves at a speed of 400 kilometres per hour. Immediately after receiving such a message, it is transmitted to the Hypothalamus, which in turn transmits it to the nervous system, to the medulla of the adrenal in the kidneys. The secretion of the four types of hormones starts shortly, which makes the body sick. First of all, adrenaline and non-adrenaline secretions are released into the body. These hormones, which provide us strength to fight or run, are produced automatically, whenever we feel anger, hatred, jealousy, lust, greed and wrath. Thereafter, glucose is released from the liver to provide energy for activities such as fighting and running. Following this the heartbeat rises to increase the flow of blood to provide strength in the body. Water from the skin and lips too are drawn into the blood. Many people experience dryness of the mouth after anger and feel thirsty. The skin becomes pale and the throat dries up.

Frequent anger and hatred produces a chemical called 'cortisol' that reduces our overall immune system. "The more unequilibrated one becomes, the more neurotransmitter substances such as acetylcholine, serotonin and epinefrin are released. These trigger production of many types of bad effects on the crucial body organs like the thyroid, adrenal cortex, digestive tracts and reproductive organs" [4] . If we are angry, or have hatred and jealousy about another person we are ready to embrace the illnesses like diabetes, headache, high-blood pressure, increased cholesterol levels in the blood and even cancer. Immunity to diseases is reduced due to excess cortisol levels in the body and one may become susceptible to illnesses such as influenza and chicken pox. Due to frequent anger and hatred the mucus membrane in the stomach dries up, which leads to the excess release of pepsin enzyme into the stomach, leading to stomach ulcers.

It is reported that frequent anger and hatred causes psychological ageing. Considering these aspects, the Buddha said: "Holding on to anger is like keeping a piece of burning coal in one's hand in the hope of throwing it on others."

The breach of any one precept induces a chain reaction and results in breach of all the five precepts one after another, if not at once.

So, we can clearly see that by observing these precepts we are not doing any favour to anybody or to the society. We observe precepts mainly for our own benefit, prosperity and happiness.

These precepts are based on the laws of the nature and have universal application. They are not restricted to any particular sect or to the followers of a particular religion. They apply to every person irrespective of his caste, creed, gender, age, domicile and era. They are beyond the limitation of time and space. Any person who wants to live a happy life has to observe these precepts. There is no exception. Therefore, the Buddha called them eternal: "*Esa Dhammo Sanantano.*" (This is the eternal law).

The second step, for the first three-and-a-half days, the students practice *Ānāpāna Sati* -observation of the natural in-coming breath, and out-going breath as it is without regulating the natural reality of the breath. This leads to the ability to develop control over our unruly mind. Mind gets concentrated and increasingly subtle, which makes it sharper and very sensitive.

The habit pattern of our mind is such that it never wants to remain stable and peaceful. It always wants to remain busy, involved in one problem or another. If we analyse the behaviour of our mind we can find that it either thinks about the events of the past or imagines the happenings in the future. Similarly, if we analyse the kind of thoughts we have, we can find that they are either pleasant or unpleasant. If the thoughts are pleasant, we want to have more of them, and so we develop craving for them, but if they are unpleasant, we want to avoid them and generate aversion for them.

The third step is the practice of *Vipassanā* by which one penetrates one's entire physical and mental structure with the clarity of insight. With *Vipassanā*, one observes the mind-matter phenomenon, the truth of the so-called 'I', the truth about the cause and effect of suffering, and the way out of this suffering. One makes this observation within the framework of the body, without any illusion, delusion, imagination, or visualisation. One observes reality as it is. There is no cult, *gurudhamma*, philosophy, dogma, rites, or rituals involved. One is not asked to observe the truth experienced by the Buddha, or the present teacher or by someone else. One observes the truth that one is directly experiencing with the framework of the body.

Importantly, the *Vipassanā* student observes the truth of this moment, as it is. The truth experienced in the previous moment, leave alone the previous second or minute, is no longer the truth. It is past. It has changed. The truth of the sensations at this moment is the reality. So, one experiences the truth of the changing reality, from one moment to another, within the framework of the body. Nature is playing its role, one just observes. One realises how difficult this is! One also realises how necessary and beneficial this is!

Soon, the *Vipassanā* practitioner experiences how the mind is blindly reacting to these bodily sensations with craving or aversion, with attachment or hatred. One experiences how this habit pattern of blind reaction to the pleasant or unpleasant reality of sensations, which is not in our control, causes a vicious cycle of suffering and misery. One also realises that only at the apparent level we are reacting to objects, situations and people in the world outside and in reality, one is constantly reacting to the sensations caused by the outside objects coming in contact with the sense doors of eyes, ears, nose, body, tongue, and mind. This is the truth of the nature, as it is, the deep- rooted habit pattern of blind reaction. This is the truth of suffering, of misery that one causes for oneself and then throws it on those around.

By training the mind to objectively observe the sensations, instead of blindly reacting to them, the *Vipassanā* meditator experiences the path leading to real happiness, the path leading to the end of suffering. Every time a negative thought or emotion arises, the meditator does not harm himself by suppressing or blindly expressing these negative feelings. Rather one enjoys the benefits of the middle path of mere observation, neither suppression nor expression. One experiences how the negative habit pattern starts weakening at the root level. When no new fuel is added to the fire, the fire gradually ebbs out. One starts experiencing real happiness in life, the happiness of a pure, peaceful mind.

The practitioner observes the various sensations in the body and realises their impermanence. This realisation purifies the mind from the defilements of craving and aversion. By practicing *Vipassanā*, the habit pattern of the mind undergoes some radical changes. The practitioner just observes the sensations without reacting to them. It is a choiceless observation. The Buddha called it *'Yathā-bhūta Jñāna Darshana'*. By observing sensations objectively and not reacting to them, the old stock of craving and aversion gets evaporated and eradicated. The less the stock of craving and aversion, the lesser is the defilement of the mind. When no craving or aversion is left and we stop generating and accumulating new *Saṅkhāra-s* of craving and aversion, the mind becomes free and pure from defilements, and the practitioner experiences the bliss of *Nibbāna*.

The practitioner also receives systematic meditation instructions several times a day, and each day's progress is explained during a taped evening discourse by Mr. Goenka. While complete silence is observed for the first nine days, on the tenth day, students resume speaking, making the transition back to a more empirical way of life. The retreat concludes on the morning of the 11th day. The retreat closes with the practice of *Metta Bhāvanā* (meditation of loving kindness or good will towards all).

Metta Bhāvanā

The practice of *Metta-Bhāvanā* (meditation of loving-kindness or good will towards all) is a meditation technique in which the purity developed during the course is shared with all. The practitioners radiate their positive energy towards all beings by wishing 'Whatsoever living beings are there, feeble or strong, long, stout or medium, short, small or large, seen or unseen, those who dwelling far or near, those who are born and those who are to be born, may all beings, without exception, be happy-minded; may all beings be well and happy; may they be full of joy and happiness; may they be full of loving kindness to each other.'

Metta Bhāvanā is also practiced to purify one's defilements of mind like-anger, jealousy, hatred and self-pity. It is to make us peaceful with the world. *Metta* has a psychological effect to stop generation of anger, hatred and jealousy. It has been proved in experiments that the best way to save a person who had fallen ill due to anger, hatred and wrath described above, is to make him practise meditation of loving-kindness. 'British scientists have proved that meditation for loving kindness restores the chemical balance in the body. Cholesterol level in the body is reduced by meditation and a person's immunity to diseases increases and he becomes healthy, if he practices meditation of loving kindness for a short time each day. Meditation of loving kindness is very good for those who are ill'[5].

Where to Practice?

Vipassanā retreats are held regularly at the permanent centres and rented sites in different countries. In addition to frequent ten-day retreats, special retreats and long retreats of 20, 30, 45 and 60 days are periodically offered for advanced students. Short courses in *Ānāpāna*, the introductory part of the *Vipassanā* technique, are regularly offered for children. The courses last for one-three days and serve children in two age groups: 8-11, and 12-15.

All retreats throughout the world are run solely on the basis of voluntary donations. No fee of any kind is charged because it is believed that the *Dhamma* is so invaluable that nobody can pay a price for it. The *Dhamma* cannot be valued in monetary terms. The retreats are financed totally by donations from students who have completed a prior retreat and wish to share the benefits they themselves received by giving donation for the students who come after them. Neither the teacher nor assistant teachers receive any remuneration - they are volunteers. This practice is consistent with the purity of the *Dhamma* tradition, whereby teaching is offered freely, free from any taint of commercialism, supported solely by donations stemming from the wholesome volitions of gratitude and generosity.

A Non-Sectarian Meditation Technique

People of any background can practice *Vipassanā*. There is no discrimination on the basis of gender, race, caste, creed, community, country of origin, socio-economic status, education etc. The only requirement is that the person should be mature and willing to practice the meditation for ten days as per the daily schedule of the *Vipassanā* centre. Once a regular ten-day course is taken under a qualified teacher, it can be practised regularly at home.

Though the technique was made popular by the Buddha and has been a part of the Buddhist tradition, it is purely non- sectarian. The *Vipassanā* meditation technique is a purely scientific technique that can be practised anywhere, across the world. It is, therefore, universal. Since it works wholly according to the laws of the nature, which apply to every person irrespective of his age, gender, race, caste, creed, country of origin and social status. It can also be called timeless. The Buddha himself taught *Dhamma* (the way, the truth, the path). He did not call his followers "Buddhists"; but referred to them as "*Dhammists*" (those who follow the truth).

The technique works on the basis that all human beings share the same problems, and that a pragmatic method that can eradicate these problems can be universally practised. From time to time, we all experience agitation, frustration and disharmony. And when we suffer, we do not keep our misery limited to ourselves;

instead, we keep distributing it to others. By practicing *Vipassanā*, we develop love and compassion and mental purity, free from defilements, which leads to liberation from suffering and miseries. We can make our own life as well as the lives of others happy and peaceful.

Some people ask how it will help the world if only a few persons are improved. How can the problems of the world, like poverty, unemployment, diseases, violence, discrimination, war, exploitation etc. be solved by a few people practicing *Vipassanā* meditation? We have to understand and realise that the individual is the key. An individual is a unit of society. Individuals make up society, societies make up nations and nations make up the world. We can share with the world only that which we have. If we have money we can share it with others. But, if we don't have even a single penny, we cannot share any money with others. Similarly, if by practicing *Vipassanā* we can make our own life happy, we can then share our happiness with others. Only happy people can make a happy world. Miserable people make a miserable world. If by practicing *Vipassanā* meditation, we can eradicate our own miseries by eradicating the mental defilements of craving and aversion, we will become happy, healthy, peaceful and harmonious. We can then distribute and share this wealth with others. By *Vipassanā* we generate love and compassion in our hearts, and by practicing *Metta Bhāvanā* we spread it to others. Thus, by practicing *Vipassanā* we not only reduce the sum- total of misery and unhappiness in the world, but we also contribute our part to the sum-total of happiness, peace and harmony in the world.

In the past millennia, we saw, and we still continue to see, how *Vipassanā* enables one to lead a happy and harmonious life. When more individuals achieve inner peace, peace is brought into homes and then in neighbourhoods, villages, towns, cities, countries and then finally across the world. When an individual learns the practical path to being a good neighbour, countries learn the art of being good neighbours. As a result, conflicts arising out of sectarian differences are overcome. *Vipassanā* unites while sectarianism divides.

We see this quintessential unifying process of peace and

harmony in the *Vipassanā* retreats worldwide. In the Dhamma (meditation) Hall during a *Vipassanā* retreat, people from every religion sit together to practice this ancient path of becoming a better human being. They follow the same code of discipline and rules to gain maximum benefit from this. Not only followers of different religions, but also various religious leaders have willingly participated in *Vipassanā* retreats, which are even held in temples, mosques, churches, and monasteries. *Vipassanā* has the capacity to transform the human mind and character. It is an opportunity awaiting all who sincerely wish to make the effort.

People of every background and every class, ranging from prisoners in jails to very high-ranking civil servants, from beggars to multimillionaires, young to very old, illiterate to very learned, and people from many different countries and backgrounds practice *Vipassanā*.

The studies conducted by the *Vipassanā* Research Institute, Igatpuri, Maharashtra, India and the *Vipassanā* International Academy, Igatpuri, Maharashtra, India reveal that this technique benefits all people. Many of its practitioners have reported that there is a marked and substantial improvement in their stamina, efficiency, both mental and physical capacity to work and take quick decisions, mental and physical health, and better interpersonal relationships. The practice of *Vipassanā* has made their lives happy, peaceful and harmonious. The uniqueness of *Vipassanā* is that any person can practice it at any time and anywhere. The results are always beneficial.

It is advisable that the technique is learnt under a qualified/trained *Vipassanā* teacher. It is not advisable to start practising it just by reading books, as one will not be able to grasp the technique properly.

Chapter 6
Buddhist Literature

Literature plays a very important role in the cultural development of human civilization. It helps the followers by providing them deep insight into the teachings of the founder of the path. The Buddhists have the most detailed and voluminous literature. The original words of the Buddha are contained in fifteen thousand pages. *Aṭṭhakathā*-s, which are commentaries based on the Buddha's original words and commentaries on them are contained in thirty-five thousand pages. Thus, the original Buddhist literature in *Pāli* is contained in fifty thousand pages. Every minute detail as to why a particular rule was framed and what its background was, is explained in *Vinaya Piṭaka.* The Buddha taught the *Dhamma* for forty-five years. Although the Buddha had not left any written records of his teachings, his disciples preserved them by memory and transmitted them orally from generation to generation. The words of the Buddha were not reduced to writing during his lifetime as the art of writing was not widely prevalent during those days. Whatever little was written, it was written with great difficulty on copper plates and the leaves of palm trees. His teachings were compiled and authenticated in the council of *Arahata Bhikkhu*-s (fully liberated monks). The first council of five hundred *Arahata Bhikkhus* was held at Rājagraha (in modern Bihar), three months after the Mahāparinibbāna of the Buddha, under the presidentship of Mahākāshyapa. Venerable Ānanda recited the *Dhamma* and Ven. Upāli recited the *Vinaya*. The first council compiled and arranged the *Pāli Tipiṭaka*, the entire body of the Buddha's teachings. Two other councils of *Arahanta*-s were held about 100 and 236 years later respectively to authenticate the original words of the Buddha because some vested interests were making attempts to pollute the pure teachings. The fourth council was held at Āluvihāra, Ceylon in 83 BC. Here the *Tipiṭaka* was, for the first time, committed to writing. The Corporate Body Of the Buddha Educational Foundation, Taipei, Taiwan, has published full *Tipitakas* in 126 volumes. The *Tipiṭaka* contain the essence of Buddha's teachings. The word *Tipiṭaka* means three baskets. These are basket of discipline (*Vinaya Piṭaka*), basket of Discourses (*Sutta- Piṭaka*) and the basket of Ultimate Realities (*Abhidhamma Piṭaka*).

Vinaya Pitaka

This is the collection of texts concerning the rules of conduct governing the daily affairs within the *Saṅgha* - the community of *Bhikkhu-s* (ordained monks) and *Bhikkhuni*-s (ordained nuns). The *Vinaya Pitaka* includes the stories behind the origin of each rule, providing a detailed account of the Buddha's solution to the question of how to maintain communal harmony within a large and diverse spiritual community.

The *Vinaya Piṭaka* consists of the following five books:

Pārājikā Pāli (Major offences)
Pācittiya Pāli Vibhanga (Minor offences)
Mahāvagga Pāli (Greater Section)
Cullavagga Pāli Khandhaka (Lesser Section)
Parivāra Pāli (Epitome of the Vinaya)

Sutta Piṭaka

Sutta Piṭaka consists mainly of instructive discourse delivered by Lord Buddha on various occasions. A few discourses, expounded by disciples such as the Venerable Sāriputta, Moggallāna and Ānanda, are incorporated and are accorded as much veneration as the words of the Buddha himself, since they were approved by him. The Sutta Piṭaka consists of the following five *Nikāyas* (Collections):

Digha Nikāya (collection of long discourses)
Majjhimā Nikāya (collection of middle-length discourses)
Saṁyutta Nikāya (collection of kindred sayings)
Aṅguttara Nikāya (collection of gradual sayings)

Khuddaka Nikāya (smaller collection)

Digha Nikāya

It is made up of thirty-four long discourses of the Buddha and divided into three divisions:

1. Silakkhandha-vagga (division concerning morality)
2. Mahāvagga (the large division)
3. Pāthika vagga (the division beginning with the discourse on Pathika, the naked ascetic)

Majjhimā Nikāya

This collection is made up of one hundred and fifty-two suttas in three books known as pannasa. The first book, *Mūlapaññāsa*, deals with the first fifty suttas in five *Vagga-s*; the second book, *Majjhimapaññāsa* consists of the second fifty suttas, also in five *vaggas*; and the last fifty-two suttas are dealt with in five *Vaggas* of the third book, *Uparipaññāsa*, which means more than fifty. The *Sutta-s* in this *Nikāya* throw much light on the social ideas and institutions of those days, and also provide general information on the economic and political life of that time.

Saṁyutta Nikāya

It is made up of seven thousand seven hundred sixty two suttas of varied length generally short, arranged in special order according to subject matter into five major divisions:

Sagātha-vagga Nidāna-vagga Khandha-vagga
Salāyatana-vagga Mahā-vagga

Each major Vagga is divided into fifty six groups known as *Samyutta-s* related-subjects grouped together.

Anguttara-nikāya

It is made up of nine thousand five hundred fifty seven short suttas, divided into eleven divisions known as *Nipāta-s*. Each *Nipata* is divided into groups called *Vagga-s* which usually contain ten suttas:

Khuddaka-nikaya

It is made up of the largest number of suttas. It contains the discourses by the Buddha and compilation of brief doctrinal notes mostly in verse, accounts of personal struggles and achievements by *theras* (Buddhist Monks) and *theris* (Buddhist Nuns) also in verse, the birth stories and the history of the Buddha.

It is divided into fifteen books:

1. Khuddaka patha (Shorter Texts)
2. Dhammapada (The Way of Truth)
3. Udana (Exclamations of Joy)
4. Itivuttaka ("Thus said" Discourses)
5. Sutta-nipata (Collected Discourses)
6. Vimana vatthu (Stories of Celestial Mansions)
7. Peta-vatthu (Stories of Petas)
8. Theragatha (Personal experiences of monks)
9. Therigatha (Personal experiences of nuns)
10. Jātaka (Birth Stories of the Bodhisatva)
11. Niddesa (Expositions)
12. Paṭisambhida (Book on Analytical Knowledge)
13. Apadāna (Lives of Arahants)
14. Buddhavaṁsa (History of the Buddha)
15. Cariyā piṭaka (Modes of Conduct)

Abhidhamma Pitaka

Abhidhamma piṭaka is the most important and most interesting of the three *Piṭaka-s*. It contains the profound philosophy of the Buddha's teachings in contrast to the simpler discourses in the *Sutta piṭaka*. *Abhidhamma*, the Higher Doctrine of the Buddha, expounds the quintessence of His profound teachings.

To the wise truth-seekers, *Abhidhamma* is an indispensable guide and an intellectual treat. It provides food for thought to original thinkers and to earnest students who wish to develop wisdom and lead an ideal Buddhist life.

While the *Sutta piṭaka* contains the conventional teaching (*vohāra-desanā*), the *Abhidhamma piṭaka* contains the ultimate teaching (*Paramattha-desanā*).

It is generally admitted by most expounders of the *Dhamma* that knowledge of the *Abhidhamma* is essential to comprehend fully the teachings of the Buddha, as it presents the key that opens the door of reality.

The *Abhidhamma piṭaka* is composed of the following works:

1.	Dhammasaṅgani	(Classification of Dhamma)
2.	Vibhaṅga	(Divisions)
3.	Dhātukathā	(Discourse of Elements)
4.	Puggalapaññatti	(The Book on Individuals)
5.	Kathāvatthu	(Points of Controversy)
6.	Yamaka	(The Book of Pairs)
7.	Paṭṭhāna	(The Book of Causal Relations)

In modern time, the most important book about the Buddha and the *Dhamma* has been written by Dr. Ambedkar titled as 'The Buddha and His *Dhamma*'. The other important book is 'Essence of Buddhism' by P. Lakshmi Narassu. Vipassanā Research Institute, Dhammagiri, Igatpuri has published 154 books about life of the Buddha and his teachings. The entire collection of the *Tipiṭaka* is available in 140 volumes.

In today's era of the Internet, there are many websites which provide information about the Buddha and his teachings. Some of these websites are given in the Annexure-I of this Book.

Notes

Chapter-1, Life of the Buddha

1. Some authors believe that Siddhāttha Gotama was born in 623 BC, Narada, *The Buddha and His Teachings*, Buddhist Missionary Society, Kualalumpur, 1988, p.1.
2. Thich Nhat Hanh, *Old Path White Clouds*, Full circle, New Delhi, 1997, "Beneath a Rose – Apple Tree", p. 45.
3. Anguttara Nikāya. 1.134.
4. Dr. B.R. Ambedkar, *Buddha and His Dhamma*, Siddhartha Publication, Mumbai – 1957. "How a Boddhisatta became the Buddha", p.19.
5. Ibid., p. 21.
6. Thich Nhat Hanh, *Old Path White Clouds*, Full circle, New Delhi, 1997, "Unborn Child", p. 68-69.
7. Ibid., p. 69.
8. Ibid., p. 69.
9. Dr. B.R. Ambedkar, *The Buddha and His Dhamma*, Siddhartha Publication, Mumbai – 1957. "How a Bodhisatta became the Buddha", p. 24.
10. Ibid, p. 25.
11. Ibid, p. 25.
12. Ibid, p. 25.
13. Ibid, p. 28.
14. Ibid, p. 29.
15. Acharya S.N. Goenka, *Was the Buddha A Pessimist*? Vipassanā Research Institute Igatpuri, July, 2001, "Happi- ness and Welfare of Many", p. 21.
16. Ibid, p. 17.

16a. Dr. B.R. Ambedkar, *The Buddha and His Dhamma*, Siddhartha Publication, Mumbai – 1957. "How a Boddhisatta became the Buddha", p. 30.

17. Ibid, p. 34.
18. Ibid, p. 35.
19. Ibid, p. 35.
20. Ibid, p. 38.
21. Ibid, p. 49.
22. Ibid, p. 55.
23. Ibid, p. 58. 23a. Ibid, p. 61-62.
24. Thich Nhat Hanh, *Old Path White Clouds*, Full Circle, New Delhi, 1998, 'Beginning Spiritual Practice", p. 94.
25. Ibid, "Forest Ascetic", p. 101.
26. Aṅguttara Nikāya, 8:20

26a. Karen Armstrong, '*Buddha*', Phoenix, London, "Enlightement", p.70.

27. Jātaka, 1: 71
28. Dr. B.R. Ambedkar, *The Buddha and His Dhamma*, "How a Bodhisatta became the Buddha", p. 74.
29. Dhamma pada: Verses 153, 154
30. Vinaya Pitaka 1.23
30a. Venerable K. Sri Dhammananda, *What Buddhists Believe*, The Corporate Body of the Buddha Educational Foundation, Taipei,1993 'His Message-Miraculous Power', p. 32-33.
31. Narada, *The Buddha and His teachings*, Buddhist Missionary Society, Kuala Lumpur,1988, "Buddha's Parinibbana", p. 244.
32. Dīgha Nikāya, 2:119
33. Thich Nhat Hanh, *Old Path White Clouds*, Full circle, New Delhi, 1997, p. 562-564.
34. Sutta – Nipāta, 5:7

Chapter-2, Preachings of the Buddha

1. Dhammapada: Verse-327. Chapter - 9 - Pāpa Vagga. Chapter - 23- Nāga Vagga.
2. Dr. B.R. Ambedkar, *Buddha and His Dhamma*, "His Place in His Dhamma," p. 218. William Hart, *The Art of Living – Vipassanā Meditation as Taught by S.N. Goenka*, Vipassanā Research Institute, Igatpuri, 1991 "The Search" p. 21.
3. Saṁyutta Nikāya, Mahāvagga Saṁyutta Pāli. William Hart, *The Art of Living–Vipassanā Meditation as Taught by S.N. Goenka,* Vipassanā Research Institute, Igatpuri, 1991 "The Root of the Problem", p. 55.
4. Thich Nhat Hanh, *Old Path White Clouds*, Full Cicle, New Delhi – 1997, "Bamboo Forest", p. 194.
5. Dhammapada: Verse – 119, 120.
6. Dhammapada: Verse – 113, Chapter-8, "Sahassa Vagga".
7. Dhammapada: Verse – 114, Chapter-8, "Sahas Vagga", 8:13.
8. Dhammapada: Verse – 173, Chapter-13, "Lok Vagga", 13:5.
9. Dhammapada: Verse – 213, Chapter-16, "Piya Vagga".
10. Dr. B.R. Ambedkar, *Buddha and His Dhamma,* "His Enemies", p. 355.
11. Narada, *The Buddha and His Teachings*, Buddhist Missionary Society, Kuala Lumpur, 1988, "The Buddha's Chief Opponents and Supporters", p. 159.
12. Dīgha Nikāya – III.
13. Suttanipāta Stanza – 33.
14. Majjhimā Nikāya– I, p. 85.
15. Saṁyutta Nikāya – III, p. 266.
16. Saṁyutta Nikāya – IV, p. 336.
17. Aṅguttara Nikāya – III, p. 279.
18. Saṁyutta Nikāya – I, p. 90.
19. Kancha Ilaiah, *God as Political Philosopher: Buddha's Chal- lenge to Brahminism*, Samya, Kolkata, 2001 "Women", p. 185.
20. Ibid, p. 192, 193.

21. Narada, *The Buddha and His Teachings*, Buddhist Missionary Society, Kualalumpur, 1988. "Characteristics of Buddhism- Buddhism and women", p. 313.
22. Kancha Ilaiah, *God as Political Philosopher: Buddha's Chal- lenge to Brahminism*, Samya, Kolkata, 2001 "Women", p. 195.
23. Dīgha Nikāya – I.
24. Dīgha Nikāya – I.
25. Dr. B.R. Ambedkar, *Buddha and His Dhamma,* Part IV, "His Sermon", p. 405.
26. Ibid, p. 406.
27. Ibid, p. 401, 402.

Chapter-3, The Essence of Dhamma

1. Dhamapada: XX 4 (276)
2. Thich Nhat Hanth, *Old Path White Clouds*, Full Circle, New Delhi, 1997 "Where will the Buddha Go ?", p. 467.
3. Narada, *The Buddha and His Teachings*, Buddhist Missionary Society, Kualalumpur, 1988. "The Buddha's Chief Opponents and Supporters, Parami Perfections", p. 576.
4. Saṁyutta Nikāya, 2.4.249. 5. Ibid, 2.4251.
6. Buddhadasa P. Kritisinghe, *Buddhism and Science*, Motilal Banarsidas Publishers Pvt. Ltd., New Delhi, 1984, "Introduction", p. 5.
7. Ibid, p. 9.
8. Aṅguttara Nikāya, 3:65.
9. Dīgha Nikāya, Sīlakkahndha Pāli.
10. Brahmajāla-sutta, Majjhimā Nikāya, 74, Dīghanakha Sutta.
11. Narada, *The Buddha and His Teachings*, Buddhist Mission- ary Society, Kualalumpur, 1988. "The Dhamma", p. 286.
12. Dhammapada: XII, 9 (165)
13. Dhammapada: XIV, 5 (183). 14. Ibid., I.17 & 18.
15. Majjhimā Nikāya, 117, MahāSattavipaka, Sutta.
16. Dhammapada: XX.4 (276).
17. Dhammapada: I. 1&2.
18. Dhammapada: XX 4 (276).
19. William Hart, *The Art of Living – Vipassanā Meditation as Taught by S.N. Goenka*, Vipassanā Research Institute, Igatpuri, 1991, 'The training of concentration', p. 74.
20. Dhammapada: I. Yamak Vaggo.

Chapter-4, The Law of Dependent Origination

1. Sayagyi U Ba khin Journal, 1998, p. 255.
2. Saṁyutta Nikāya, Nidāna Saṁyutta, Paticcasamuppadā sutta.
3. Majjhimā Nikāya.38, Mahātaṇhāsankhāya Sutta.
4. Ibid.
5. Thich Naht Hanh, *Old Path white clouds*, Full circle, New Delhi-1997, "Pippala Leaf[", p.115.

Chapter-5, Vipassanā

1. Saṁyutta Nikāya, 3:1.8.
2. Therigāthā, Aṭṭhaka Nipāta Gāthā No. 200.
3. Theragāthā, Gāthā No.139.
4. Buddhadasa P. Kirthisinghe; Buddhism and Science, Motilal Banarasidas, Delhi, 1984, "Buddhist Meditation and Bioscience", p. 56-57.
5. Ānanda, *Bhagwan Buddha: Dhamma Sar Va Dhammacharya*, Samruddha Bharat Publication, Mumbai, 2004, "Vipassanā", p. 129.

Chapter - 6, Buddhist Literature

1. Narada, *The Buddha and His Teachings*, Buddhist Missionary Society, Kuala Lumpur 1988, "What is Buddhism", p. 271.

Glossary

Included in this list are *Pāli* terms that appear in the text as well as some other terms of importance in the teaching of the Buddha.

Ānāpāna : Respiration. *Ānāpāna – sati* awareness of respiration.

Anatta : No self, egoless, without essence, without substance. One of the three basic characteristics of phenomena, along with *anicca* and *dukkha*.

Anicca : Impermanent, ephemeral, changing. One of the three basic characteristics of phenomena, along with *anatta* and *dukkha*.

Arahanta/ arahata : Liberated being. One who has destroyed all impurities of the mind.

Āsana : The correct position for yogic meditation, with straight back and crossed legs.

Bhikkhu : (Buddhist) monk; meditator. Feminine form *bhikkhuni*

Buddha : Enlightened person. One who has discovered the way to liberation, has practiced it, and has reached the final goal by his own effort.

Bodhisatta : A man or woman who is destined to achieve Enlightenment. Sanskrit: *Bodhisatva*.

Dhamma : Phenomenon; object of mind; nature; natural law; law of liberation, i.e. teaching of an Enlightened Person (Buddha).

Dhammānupassanā : Observation of the contents of the mind. See *Satipaṭṭhāna* (Sanskrit Dharma).

Dukkha : Suffering, dissatisfaction. One of the three basic characteristics of phenomena, along with *anatta* and *anicca*.

Gotama : Family name of the historical Buddha. (Sanskrit Gautama).

Gotami : The name of any woman belonging to the Gotama

tribe.

Iddhi : The dominion of spirit over matter; the 'miraculous; powers thought to come with proficiency in *yoga*, e.g., levitation or the ability to change shape at will.

Jhānas : State of mental absorption or trance. There are eight such states which may be attained by the practice of *samādhi*, or *samatha-bhavana*. Cultivation of them brings tranquility and bliss, but does not eradicate the deepest-rooted mental defilements.

Kalāpa : Smallest indivisible unit of matter.

Kamma : Action, specifically an action performed by oneself which will have an effect on one's future. (Sanskrit Karma).

Khandha : Heaps, bundles, lums, the constituents of the human personality in the Buddha's theory of *anatta*. The five 'heaps' are body, feelings, perception, volition and consciousness.

Kusala : The 'Skillful' or helpful states of mind and heart that Buddhists should cultivate in order to achieve Enlightenment.

Metta : Selfless love and good will. One of the qualities of a pure mind. *Metta-bhāvanā*-the systematic cultivation of *metta* by a technique of meditation.

Nibbāna : Extinction; freedom from suffering; the ultimate reality; the unconditioned.

Nikāya : Collections of discourses in the *Pāli* Canon.

Pāli : Line text. The texts recording the teaching of the Buddha; hence the language of these texts. Historical, linguistic, and archaeological evidence indicate that *Pāli* was a language actually spoken in northern India at or near the time of the Buddha. Later the texts were translated in the Sanskrit, which was exclusivetly a literary language.

Paññā : Wisdom. The third of the three trainings by which the Noble Eightfold Path is practiced (see ariya-aṭṭhangika-magga). There are three kinds of wisdom: *suta-maya* paññā- literally, "wisdom gained from listening to others," i.e., received wisdom; *cinta-mayā paññā*-wisdom gained by intellectual analysis;

and *bhavanā-mayā paññā-* wisdom developing from direct, personal experience. Of these, only the last can totally purify the mind; it is cultivated by the practice of *vipassanā-bhāvanā*.

Paṭicca-samuppāda: The Chain of Conditioned Arising; causal genesis. The process, beginning with ignorance, by which one keeps making life after life of suffering for oneself.

Pabbajjā : 'Going Forth'; the act of renouncing the world in order to live the holy life of a monk. Later, the first step in Buddhist ordination.

Parinibbāna : The 'Final *Nibbāna*'; the final rest of an enlightened person achieved at death, since he or she will not be reborn into another existence.

Sila : Morality, purity of vocal and physical actions.

Sammā-vācā : Right speech.

Sammā-kammanto: Right action.

Sammā-ājivā: Right livlihood;

Samādhi : Concentration, control of one's own mind.

Sammā-vāyāma : Right effort.

Sammā-sati : Right awareness.

Sammā-samādhi : Right concentration.

Paññā : Wisdom, insight which totally purifies the mind.

Sammā-saṅkappa: Right thought.

Sammā-diṭṭhi: Right understanding.

Ariya Sacca : Noble truth. The Four Noble Truths are (1) the truth of suffering; (2) the truth of the origin of suffering; (3) the truth of the cessation of suffering; (4) the truth of the path leading to the cessation of suffering.

Śākyamuni : 'The Sage of the Republic of Sakka', a title given to Gotama the Buddha.

Sāmkhya : Yogic concentration; meditation; one of the components of the Eightfold Path to enlightment.

Sammā Sambuddha : A Teacher of enlightment, one of whom comes to humanity every 32,000 years; Siddhāttha Gotama is the Sammā Sambuddha of our own age.

Samsāra : 'Keeping going'; the cycle of death and rebirth, which propels people from one life to the next; the transience and restlessness of mundane existence.

Saṅgha : Originally a tribal assembly, an ancient governing body in the old republics of North India; later a sect professing the *Dhamma* of a particular teacher; finally, the Buddhist Order of *Bhikkhu*-s.

Saṅkhāra : 'Formation'; the formative element in kamma, which determines and shapes one's next existence.

Sutta : A religious discourse. Sanskrit; *Sutra*.

Taṇhā : Literally, "thirst". Includes both craving and its reverse image of aversion. The Buddha identified *taṇhā* as the cause of suffering in his first-sermon, the "Discourse setting in Motion the Wheel of *Dhamma*" (*Dhamma*-cakkappavattana-sutta). In the Chain of Conditioned Arising, he explained that *Taṇhā* originates as a reaction to sensation.

Tathāgata : Literally "thus-gone" or "thus-came" One who by walking on the path of reality has reached the ultimate reality, i.e., an Enlightened person. The term by which the Buddha commonly referred to himself.

Tipiṭaka : Literally, "three baskets" The three collections of the teachings of the Buddha, namely: (1) *Vinaya-piṭaka*- the collection of monastic discipline; (2) *Sutta-piṭaka*- the collection of discourses; (3) *Abhidhamma-piṭaka*- the collection of higher teaching," i.e., systematic philosophical exposition of the *Dhamma*. (Sanskrit Tripitaka).

Upādāna : 'Clinging,' attachment; it is etymologically related to upadi, fuel.

Uposatha : The days of fasting and abstinence in the Buddhist tradition.

Vassavas : The retreat during the monsoon rains from June to September.

Vinaya : The monastic code of the Buddhist Order; one of the 'Three Baskets' of the *Tipiṭaka*.

Vedanā : Sensation. One of the four mental aggregates or processes, along with *viññāna*, *sañña*, and *saṅkhāra*. Described by the Buddha as having both mental and physical aspects; therefore, *vedana* offers a means to examine the totality of mind and body. In the Chain of Conditioned Arising, the Buddha explained that *taṇṇhā*, the cause of suffering, originates as a reaction to *vedana*. By learning to observe *vedanā* objectively, one can avoid any new reactions of craving or aversion, and can experience directly within oneself the reality of impermanence (anicca). This experience to liberation of the mind. *Vedanāupassanā* – observation of sensations within the body.

Vinñāna : Consciousness, cognition. One of the four mental aggregates or processes, alongwith *sanna, vedana* and *saṅkhāra*.

Vipassanā : Introspection, insight that totally purifies the mind. Specifically, insight into the impermanent nature of mind and body.

Vipassanā-bhāvanā : The systematic development of insight through the meditation technique of observing the reality of oneself by observing sensations within the body.

Yathā-bhūtā : Literally, "as it is." Reality.

Yathā-bhūtā-ñāna-dassana : Wisdom arising from seeing the truth as it is and not as it ought to be.